Corpsewood:

The Eyewitness

Account

Shannon West

Susan E Scott

Teresa Hudgins

Corpsewood: The Eyewitness Account

Copyright © 2015 Shannon West, Susan E Scott,

Teresa Hudgins

About the Book You Have Purchased

Prologue

Whatever happened in that secluded home was the devil's work. But who were the real devils?

Dead Horse Road on the way to Corpsewood

The truth of a crime is not always easy to unravel, especially after many years have passed. Such is the case with the killings of Charles Scudder and Joseph Odom, two openly gay men living on an isolated property near Summerville, Georgia, in December of 1982.

1

CORPSEWOOD: THE EYEWITNESS ACCOUNT

Obscured by layers of speculation, innuendo and lies, what actually happened on December 12, 1982 is elusive. Only one thing is certain—the murders at Corpsewood were vicious and completely devoid of human compassion.

The ruins of the estate called Corpsewood are the only thing left, hidden deep in the Georgia woodlands. The grounds, appropriately and ironically named, are there for the morbidly curious and those seeking signs of the paranormal. The buildings that once stood are only brick remnants, covered in ivy and slowly being absorbed back into the woods, and many strange tales have been told about the place by those brave enough to wander down the rutted dirt road and venture deep into the woods to explore the grounds. Stories of hauntings persist, and even now, some thirty-three years after what happened there, nearly everyone in the area calls it "the devil worshippers' house".

Part of the ruins at Corpsewood still standing with
Charles Scudder and Joey Odom's original brickwork

According to topographical maps, Taylor's Ridge, where Charles Scudder and Joseph Odom bought the land to build their home, is the most northwestern ridge in the state of Georgia and is approximately forty miles in length. To the west the ridge is bordered by the Cumberland Plateau region and to the north Taylor's Ridge becomes White Oak Mountain at Ringgold Gap. The ridge lies halfway between Rome and Summerville, Georgia, is a well-traveled area, and populated by around 23,000 residents, spread out over its length and breadth. Scudder and Odom purchased forty acres on Taylor's Ridge in June of 1975, hauled a travel trailer from their old home in Chicago, and began building their home on the property.

Bound on three sides by the Chattahoochee National Forest, the home was secluded and private. Following the on-line directions to the spot, it's easy to get lost unless you use the map coordinates. From Georgia Highway 27 North you turn onto Mountain View Road, just outside of Trion. The road soon turns to dirt and it's necessary to travel almost to the top of the mountain before making an extremely sharp turn to the right, where the road splits. This road goes to the entrance of Corpsewood, which is marked only by boulder with the scrawled inscription CW. The narrow logging type road that leads back to the site is an easy enough walk, about a quarter of a mile long. Trees are down across the road in some places and the road was barred by large puddles of water in deep ruts on the day we went there. Still, it's a peaceful, beautiful area.

According to various websites, including *The Okie Legacy, Cherokees in Chattooga*, by NW Okie and Sadie, Richard Taylor was a mixed-race Cherokee, born on Feb. 10, 1788 in a Cherokee settlement in what is now Monroe County, Tennessee.[1] Both his British and his Cherokee relatives were of some prominence. And Taylor himself, at his home in Taylor's Gap, grew prosperous and gained influence among the Cherokee. In addition to large log inn at the gap, Taylor operated a grist mill and a saw mill, and kept a farm. The inn, an impressive log structure, sat on a rise overlooking Chickamauga Creek for many years. Taylor lost his home and land during the Cherokee Indian Removals, and in 1838, was a participant of the "trail of tears."

The land where Scudder and Odom built their home is not too

close to the gap where Taylor had his outpost, but it's just as isolated and hard to locate—which is how the men wanted it to be. They came to the area seeking privacy and a respite from the "rat race" of the big city. They enjoyed their seclusion and didn't have any electricity or running water and certainly no telephone. Back in 1982, in the days before cell phones and computers, they were truly cut off from the outside world. Their friend, Raymond Williams, who lived nearby, decided to pay the men a visit in the early afternoon of a cold Sunday on December 12, 1982, to inform the men that another of their friends lay on his death bed in a local hospital. He stayed to talk with them for about a half an hour and then left, promising to return and let them know if the friend passed away. It was to be the last time he ever saw his friends alive.

The following Tuesday, December 14, Roy Hood, the mutual friend of Raymond Williams and the men, died in a Rome hospital. The next morning, Raymond made the journey to Corpsewood to tell Scudder and Odom of the death.

He turned off onto the small road that led to Corpsewood called Dead Horse Road because Charles Scudder had found a dead horse stretched across it when he first came to the property years earlier. Williams drove slowly down the narrow, rutted driveway, some quarter of a mile back into the dense woods. As he arrived in the clearing where the house stood, he saw that Scudder's black Jeep was gone, but he thought Joey might be inside, so he got out of his truck and went to the green kitchen door of the home. As he got closer, he saw that it was standing open on that cold morning and

5

most alarming of all, he saw several bullet holes in the window pane. The heavy steel door that closed over the kitchen door was also standing wide open.

Alarmed, he stepped slowly backward and almost ran toward his car, never even setting foot inside the house. He took off down the narrow road as fast as he could and traveled to the bottom of the Ridge to the Mountain View community, where he called the sheriff's office to report what he had seen.

The sheriff's office in Chattooga County was all too familiar with the forty-acre estate in the woods. Officers had patrolled the area often in the past, due to several complaints to the sheriff about the men living there on the Ridge. A popular sheriff, Gary McConnell had taken over the department after his father died in office in 1967. The sheriff had tried to bring charges against the two men in the past, but was told by prosecutors to back off. "They came here six years ago," he would tell reporters later, speaking of Scudder and Odom, "and they made it clear they wanted to be left alone. Over the years they made some friends. It was pretty well-known they were devil worshippers."

The responding officers already knew the way to the house, and Chattooga County deputies Greg Latta and Charles Starkey made their way down the Dead Horse Road on that cold, windy day not long after Williams had made his call. Latta was the first one to enter the house and saw the bodies of Charles Scudder and Joseph Odom on the floor of the kitchen. He also spotted two huge dogs lying by a stove and pulled his weapon. Latta would say later that he'd heard about the dogs belonging to the men, two English mastiffs, and he'd heard they were vicious. When his eyes adjusted to the dim interior, he soon realized the dogs were dead, too, still lying beside a wood stove in the kitchen. Latta and Starkey searched the house, but found no other bodies. They could see that the house had been ransacked and called both Sheriff Gary McConnell and Investigator Tony Gilleland to come to the scene. The sheriff called in for forensics help from the State Crime Lab and also put in a call to the Georgia Bureau of Investigation.

It had been four days since the murders, so the smell of death filled the house as investigators combed over every square inch for evidence. The bodies of the two men remained on the floor of their home, stepped over by investigators, measured and photographed from every angle. The lawmen found little significant evidence, though they collected many items they deemed "suspicious." At one point they found some disturbed ground on the side of the house and thought they'd discovered fresh graves. Later, when they dug the area up, they found nothing.

They also found a stash of long, rambling letters from a prisoner at Attica State Prison in New York along with some other letters. Authorities speculated at one point that perhaps the killings were the work of one of these prisoners. Later investigators would learn that Scudder had told friends he was planning on building a halfway house for prisoners at Corpsewood. Dozens of letters from prisoners were found inside the house, all addressed to Dr. Scudder. Investigators also found three vials of clinical LSD-25 in Dr.

Scudder's desk and then speculated that drugs may have been a motive for the killings. Later the GBI would say the vials had "no evidential value."

Crime scene photo of the interior of Corpsewood, showing the ransacked rooms

Investigators were fascinated and repelled by what they found upstairs in the bedrooms. A GBI agent, Brad Bonnell, told a reporter who asked about it, "There are occult items, homosexual pornography, and a large canopied bed with a vulture over it and whips and chains."

The bodies of Scudder and Odom were removed from the house that evening in black body bags. The dogs were removed as well in the back of a pickup truck and all were taken down the mountain.

Autopsies on Scudder and Odom were performed at the Summerville Funeral Home later that same night.

Late in the afternoon or early evening of that day, investigators received a call from a local teenaged girl who claimed to have been an eyewitness to the murders. They were shocked when she told them she'd seen the whole thing, knew who the murderers were, and was ready to tell her story. She told them her name was Teresa Hudgins.

The officers who spoke to her were shocked by her testimony and that of a man named Joey Wells, another eyewitness to the crime, as chilling then as it still is today. Both were immediately given polygraph tests, walked back through the scene by investigators and interviewed numerous times by members of the sheriff's department and the Georgia Bureau of Investigation. But through it all, their testimony remained the same.

In the days following the killings, many curious residents of the county trooped through the crime scene, hoping to see the signs of devil worship and the strange, perverted sexual practices that were hinted at by the investigators. At one point, seven local preachers were paraded through the grounds to see the scene of the crime.

Speculative and downright defamatory remarks to the media made by certain members of law enforcement involved in the case, as well as by the murderers themselves, have muddied the waters since the crimes were first discovered and have led to wild speculation and rumors over the years. Ghost hunters, seekers of the paranormal, and the just plain curious still visit the site on a regular basis. On the last occasion the authors visited the site, they met with no less than three sets of other visitors on the mountain. The authors were warned more than once to "be careful up here. It can be dangerous. Be sure not to come up here at night."

In recent years, social media sites have been created to explore the nature of Corpsewood, and some of them, like the Facebook page, *Corpsewood Manor, a Castle in the Woods*, present a balanced and sympathetic view of the victims. This site is to be highly commended for its even-handed presentation of the facts, and its attempts to educate the public as to what actually happened there.

Other websites, however, try to sensationalize the crime scene and print rumor as if it were fact. Some people on these other sites claim to know the "real story" of what happened that night, claiming to be related to the murderers or to know the eyewitnesses. Some even try to vilify the victims and the eyewitnesses and exonerate and make excuses for the murderers.

Whatever happened in that secluded home built by the Scudder and Odom with their own hands was, indeed, the devil's work. But who were the real devils? Who were the killers and what was their true motive? Why did they bring along witnesses to their bloody crime? Who were these witnesses and why were they there that night? And what was the nature of the men who were killed that night—were they depraved devil-worshippers as so many have claimed, or were they simply men trying to find sanctuary in the home they'd built themselves? The questions remain and the mystery has only deepened over the intervening years.

The story of the night of the murder was told to the authorities over thirty years ago by Teresa Hudgins, that young teenaged girl, and we have reproduced her depiction of events here in her own words—her first recounting of the incident since 1982. What was the truth of that night? Only four people left alive really know what happened in that prophetically named house in the North Georgia hills, no matter what others might claim. The two murderers, still sitting in prison, have their self-serving stories. The other eyewitness has left the area. Only one of the eyewitnesses, the former Teresa Lynn Hudgins, is stepping forward again to tell the truth, to tell not only what she saw that night, but what led her to be there in that house, and what has happened to her since she testified in 1982.

She was the only one of the eyewitnesses who had the courage to step forward voluntarily to testify to what she saw, and the only one to receive a plaque from law enforcement commending her for her courage.

Plaque given to Teresa Hudgins by the Georgia Sheriff's

Association

Teresa's story is as compelling today as it was all those years ago. Her account is both chilling and heartbreaking.

Chapter One

"I longed for a family..."
--Teresa Hudgins

Childhood home of Teresa Hudgins

One day last fall, the former Teresa Hudgins was taking a friend of hers, Emily, to lunch at a local restaurant. She had been a caregiver for the friend's brother at one time, and they still got together occasionally to catch up on each other's life. As they were eating, another friend of Emily's stopped by the table. This man stood beside the table to talk to them and showed them a picture of a home he'd recently built in the North Carolina mountains. He casually mentioned that his wife was a professional writer and liked to go up to the home to work on her books.

On an impulse, Teresa gave him her phone number and asked him to give it to his wife. "I may have a story she'd be interested in," she told him.

The wife in question was one of the authors. Shannon West is her pen name and she is *no relation* to any of the parties involved. West actually had never heard the story of Corpsewood before, because when it happened and for several years afterward, she was living in Germany while her husband was stationed overseas. However, once she spoke with Teresa, she was totally fascinated by both the facts of the terrible crime and by the courage it took for an eighteen-year-old girl to not only survive that awful night, but to face down the killers and their supporters in the months to come through three separate, exhausting trials.

West's co-writer, Susan E. Scott, wrote another true-crime book about a murder in the local area several years before and was enlisted to help write the story. She was living in Rome, Georgia, in 1982 and remembered hearing of the crime on nearby Taylor's Ridge. She'd heard of the story as that of "the devil-worshippers" and didn't know what had really happened there, but like West, she was interested in the events and was anxious to meet an actual eyewitness to the murders.

Teresa is a tiny thing, only five feet two and an attractive, intelligent woman with a vibrant personality. It's easy to picture her as that young girl back in 1982, and the terror and vulnerability she must have felt as she witnessed the murders, not knowing if the gun would next be turned on her, and wanting desperately to survive that night and get back home to her daughter.

Teresa's version of that night, as told to the authors, was not vastly different from the other accounts that have appeared in newspapers and various internet blogs and ghost hunter sites, except for a few significant, chilling, and notable exceptions. These exceptions make her story well worth the retelling. In addition, little has been told about Teresa's life both before and after that night, and how she came to be an eyewitness to such a shocking crime, which is a fascinating history in itself.

This is not a story about hauntings or an attempt to sensationalize what happened. The authors, in collaboration with Teresa Hudgins, instead decided that it was time to tell the remarkable story of exactly who Charles Scudder and Joseph Odom were, unfiltered by the prejudices and misunderstandings of 1982 rural, conservative law enforcement. And it's time to tell the story of Teresa Hudgins, one filled with abandonment, personal loss, heartache, and ultimate courage, leading perhaps inevitably to Teresa's part in the tragic events of that dark, long-ago December night.

To understand the nature of the victims and the killers and to understand Teresa Hudgins' role in the events that unfolded that night at Corpsewood, along with those that came in the aftermath, it's necessary to go back to the beginning.

As told to the authors by Teresa Hudgins:

I was born August 21, 1964, in Crisp County, Georgia to Shirley Hudgins. My mother, born on April 13, 1939, was unmarried at the time of my birth, and had five other children, mostly by different fathers. Shirley Hudgins became unable to care for her children, so when I was only a baby, all her children were taken away by family members. I was taken by my grandparents for a while, but they couldn't keep me. I was kind of "passed around" to various family members for a several months and then, at one point, was given back to my grandparents.

They were unable to have me with them for long and were going to have to put me in foster care, but my mother's sister and her husband stepped in and said they'd take me in. They came to get me and take me back to their home in Chattooga County in northwest Georgia when I was about six months old. I was never formally adopted by them, but they did provide a home for me.

I don't remember much about my early childhood. As a matter of fact, I have gaps in my memories of those early days, possibly because of emotional trauma and stress. As a very young child, only five years old, something horrible happened to me that I don't talk about that to this day. Some other memories do stand out in my mind as fresh and as clear as the day they happened. For example, the day I learned that the family I thought I belonged to wasn't mine at all.

At this point in my life, I went by the last name of my aunt and uncle, and I thought they were my mother and father. I was never told any differently. I clearly remember the day I found out they weren't my parents at all. I got home from school one day when I was about seven or eight years old, and I remember walking down the long driveway to my house. Like most children, I was hungry after school and wanted a snack. I remember going straight to the kitchen and standing at the refrigerator. I decided on a piece of bologna, the kind with the red bands that go around them, and I reached for a piece.

I was face first in the refrigerator when the woman that I thought of as my grandmother came into the kitchen. This woman was "Mammy," my father's mother. Without warning, she grabbed me by the back of the neck, pulled me around and pushed me against the refrigerator door with her arm pressed against my throat. She seemed furious and I was confused, not knowing what I could have done to make her so angry. She said, "What are you doing eating this food? It doesn't belong to you. You're not even a Milam—you're a Hudgins!"

I was totally shocked. I don't even remember what I said or did, but I know I was devastated to find out that the man and woman I knew as my parents were actually my aunt and uncle. I didn't even remember my real mother and had no knowledge of her. I don't remember exactly what happened after that. I must have cried and gone to talk to the woman I thought of as my mother about it, to ask her if it was really true. Soon the truth was verified, and the shock of that moment still resonates with me today.

Mammy, then, was the first one to tell me that my last name was really Hudgins, and to let me know that I didn't belong in my uncle's family. I was crushed by the way she spoke to me and by the truth of what she said. After that, I don't think I ever had a true sense of belonging or being a part of that family. It wasn't really the fault of my "foster" parents, though they weren't particularly affectionate to me then or ever. I will always appreciate the fact that they gave me a place to live, fed me and clothed me. My life could have been much worse. I have always thought of them as my parents.

As for my real mother, I was taken by relatives to see her when I was five years old, I've been told, but I don't remember the visit. Apparently, I wouldn't have anything to do with her, which makes sense, because I certainly didn't know her at all.

I went back to see her when I was sixteen years old, around 1980. I was about to become a mother myself and I asked my uncle to take me to south Georgia where she was living in the small town of Rochelle. I wanted to see her, to see what she looked like, and find out who my real father was. I wanted to be able to tell my child one day who her family was, and I wanted to find out for myself. I was angry at my mother for giving me away, and for giving away my brothers and sisters (whom I had never met at that point). I remember standing outside as she came out on the porch to talk to me. She asked me to come in, but I was very young and very angry. I refused and told her I just needed to get some answers from her. She didn't tell me much, and I left, still not knowing who my father was, or why she did the things she did. I wouldn't see her again until the spring of 1996.

By April of 1996, I had three children, with the two youngest just six and two years old, and I wanted to know more about my real mother and father. I had a deep yearning to know them both, and I no longer held any grudges against my mother. I just needed answers. I needed to know why.

I took her a bouquet of flowers, and this time we didn't stand outside. She finally told me who my father was. She said I was the result of an affair she'd had with a married man. She told me she had another child with him too, a boy, who would be my full brother. It was the first time I knew about him, and I got in touch with him that same day, April 5, 1996. I was really happy to get to finally meet him.

He was handsome and sweet and I loved him right away. We just seemed to click, like we'd known each other our whole lives. He had been adopted and had his own family, but he'd been searching for his biological family too, just as I had.

We don't live close to each other but we keep up with each other through social media. The last I heard from him, he was no longer in contact with our father.

My mother also told me that day where my father lived. It was one of the most amazing things I learned, because I found out I had passed right by my father's house many times. I needed to connect with him. I had a need to see him, to see if I looked like him, if my children looked like him. I wanted to meet him face to face, to see who he was and let him see who I was. I wanted him to meet my children.

I contacted him and arranged a place to meet him in the small village where both my parents lived. He claimed, when I first spoke to him, that he never knew of my existence. I was visiting with my mother and I had my two small children with me. We met him at the tiny police station in town, talked for awhile, and then I told him I had to go. At that point, he looked over at my kids and pulled out his wallet to try to give me money. (He knew that my mother's house where we were spending the night was really small and little more than a shack, so he was giving me money for a motel). I said no. I told him I didn't want anything from him—I just wanted to meet him. He didn't really give my children any other special attention besides that.

We talked for a while and then I left to go back to my mother's house. On the way out of town the next day, I passed his house. Something made me pull into the driveway and go knock on the door. I guess I just wanted to say goodbye and tell him it had been nice to meet him. When he saw me there, he said, "Well, you might as well come in and meet everybody."

I started to back away, but he pulled the door open wider. I met some of his family that day, who until then didn't know I existed either. These strangers, who were actually my half-brothers and sisters and other relatives, were very friendly to me and my kids after they got over their shock at who I was. I stayed for an hour or so talking to them. For over a year after that, several of them wrote to me, and I began to feel a little like I was becoming part of their family. Then, as quick as it all started, it came to a stop. The letters stopped coming—I never knew why, because I never asked them for anything. I only wanted to know them. I never heard from any of

them again, including my father, though I continued to visit my
mother when I could until she passed away in 2001.

As I've already said, I don't have many memories of my
childhood, but by the time I was a teenager, and like most other girls
my age, I'd discovered boys. Maybe I was looking for affection. I'm
not sure. When I started dating the man who would be my first
husband, I was fifteen and he was twenty-two years old. This man,
whom I'll just call E, had a large, close-knit family that I loved being
a part of. They included me in everything and I thought I was in love.
I'm sure I was, as much as a fifteen-year-old can be, but it was too
much, too soon. I was allowed to stay there with that twenty-two-
year-old man by both his parents and my own. I became pregnant by
the age of sixteen. I was so happy for a while because I thought I
finally had my own family, a place to belong.

Of course, that happiness didn't last. Not only was I way too
young, I still hadn't found out who I was. Looking back on things, I
guess maybe he was too young too. And even though I longed for a
family, what I really wanted was my own family—my own mother,
father, brother and sisters. I wanted to have that sense of belonging
that E. had with his family and that I saw in other people's lives. I'd
never had any of that. For a time I thought that if I could put myself
into that family of E's it would help. I loved my husband and my
child, and my child helped to fill that void in my life, but I still had
no real sense of belonging. Maybe I could have eventually found
happiness there, but it wasn't to be.

A short time later, I painfully discovered that the marriage vows

21

had been broken by my husband, and after that, things between us were never the same. I won't go into the details of what happened, except to say it was a total surprise and hurt me a great deal, and after that I stopped being a good little wife. I left him, taking my child with me. I lived with some friends, and after a time, I began to date again.

On the night of December 12, 1982, when I was eighteen years old, I was asked to go on a date with a young man named Joey Wells. I remember thinking how cute Joey was and how interested I was in him. He was about my age and tall with dark hair and a little moustache, and he seemed really nice. Now after all these years have passed, I don't remember exactly how we met.

In testimony to Special Agent C.W. Johnson, Sheriff Gary McConnell and ADA Ralph Van Pelt, Joey Wells would say that earlier on the day of December twelfth, Tony West and Kenneth Avery Brock sold Teresa a kerosene heater. Teresa was slightly acquainted with Avery Brock from seeing him around the small community. Joey Wells was with them and set up a date with Teresa for later that evening.

When it came time for the date, Joey's mama, Myra, came to pick me up, because Joey's car was broken down and he was still working on it. I remember Joey was standing outside when we pulled up outside his house. He had two men with him. I knew one of them, Avery Brock, a little, but I didn't know the other man with them. He was older than we were, and I felt a little nervous of him. Joey told me he wasn't able to get his car going so we would go riding around

22

with his uncle, Tony West and Avery Brock, West's friend and roommate.

Immediately, I felt uneasy about going with them. My first instinct was to say no, and I've wished so many times I'd done just that. Joey was nice, and I wanted to spend a few hours with him, so I talked myself into it. But I remember my instincts firing wildly, telling me not to get in the car with those three men. I was afraid to go, and I should have paid attention to that little voice deep inside me. I want to tell all the young people who might be reading this that if that little voice inside you tells you not to do something, please listen. It just may be your guardian angels and God's way of protecting you from something horrific.

I didn't listen to mine, and because of that, I was taken up to the mountain that night to witness something horrible.

Chapter Two

"People often fantasize about trying out different lifestyles,
but few actually change the way they live."
—Charles Scudder

Joey Odom on left with Charles Scudder and Beelzebub circa 1981
Before describing the actual murders of Charles Scudder and
Joseph Odom, it's important to understand, if we can, just who the

victims were. And considering how much the lifestyle of Charles Scudder and Joey Odom came under fire after their murders, it's interesting to speculate on the lives of these two men, unaltered by prejudice and misconceptions. Where did they come from and what were they doing living up on Taylor's Ridge?

Apparently the sheriff of Chattooga County had some difficulty locating any of the two men's relatives after their deaths. He told the reporters from the Chicago Tribune in a news article in that paper that "the man's life (referring to Charles Scudder) is a mystery." Yet there is a great deal of information about Charles Scudder readily available for anyone who cares to search a bit. Less is known about Joey Odom's life, but he seemed to have lived quietly after about 1959 and was content to be Charles' companion and helpmate, rather than work outside the home. At the time he moved in, Charles Scudder was recently separated from his wife and was raising two of their four children.

Charles Scudder worked in Chicago as an associate professor for the Loyola University of Chicago Institute for Mind, Drugs, and Behavior. He was described by his former professor and colleague from Chicago, Dr. Alexander Karczmar, as being somewhat "eccentric," though there was no doubt that Scudder was a brilliant man. In an interview years after the incidents that occurred at Corpsewood, Karczmar described his former student, friend, and co-writer as a person "believing in the unity of the universe." At times Scudder dyed his hair either purple or red, and he even kept a pet monkey for a while. Scudder was also an accomplished harp player and had been invited to play with the Chicago Symphony Orchestra. He was a self-taught musician and had purchased a beautiful gold-plated harp, which he kept in his home. The harp was rumored to be quite valuable.[2]

Scudder once described his house in Chicago as "an old mansion in a decaying residential area…it was like a mausoleum, a tomb."[3] He bought the old mansion on West Adams Street in Chicago and filled it with baroque furniture he had bought when the Balaban and Katz Chicago Theatre was liquidating furniture. When he bought his furniture, he also purchased some old props from the theater, like human skulls and other paraphernalia from old theater productions. He kept many of these items in his house and took them with him to Georgia.

Charles Scudder was the son of Charles Morrison Scudder and Eleanor Edith Lee. He was born in Wauwatosa, Wisconsin on October 6, 1926. In the 1940s he studied at Oberlin College and was involved with the school's drama program. He took one of the lead roles in his school's 1945 production of *Candida* and did graduate work at Loyola University.

He married Helen Kilbourne Hayslette on September 10, 1946 in St. Joseph, Berrien, Michigan. He was then about twenty years old. Helen was born in Chicago, Illinois, and they had studied together at Oberlin College. Their marriage soon ended in divorce.

Charles Scudder married the former Bourtai Bunting in 1949. They were married in 1949, and their first child, Saul, was born in October of 1950, with more children following in 1951, 1952 and

1953. In 1940, Bourtai Bunting is listed on the census as living in Eau Claire, Wisconsin, with her mother and siblings. She was then eight years old, so Bourtai would have still been quite young when they married, only seventeen. She was eighteen when their first child was born. Bourtai was the daughter of a famous but eccentric British modernist poet, Basil Bunting. She was given her unusual name after a Persian poem her father admired. She was born abroad, but her American-born mother brought her and her siblings back home when she left her British husband in 1937 and returned to Wisconsin.

After she and Charles had four sons together—Saul, Gideon, Fenris, and Ahab Scudder, Charles and Bourtai Scudder separated in 1959. The next time she is mentioned in records is in 1960 when the state of Wisconsin tried to file charges against her in a dispute over monies she received for welfare support. Apparently she claimed all four children lived with her when only two of them actually did. The other two lived with Charles.

In 1959 Charles hired Joseph Odom as a housekeeper and to help him care for his children, so this timeline would make sense if he had taken two of the children to raise. Joey would have then been around twenty-one years old and Charles around thirty-three. Charles and Joseph would continue to live together for more than twenty-three years. Later when anyone asked him about whether he'd ever been married, Scudder would reply simply that yes, but his wife was dead. In fact, Scudder predeceased Bourtai, assuming she was the one he was referring to, and she and three of his sons were listed as still living at the time of his death.

Despite his marital difficulties, everyone who met Scudder remarked on his friendly, open nature. A relative of one of the authors actually met Scudder and Joey Odom in the late summer or early fall of 1982, only months before the men were killed. She said she had heard about the "devil-worshippers" and was almost afraid to meet them. But when she was introduced to them, she found both men to be very friendly and welcoming. She actually asked Scudder if he was a devil worshipper and he laughed and said no. He said he simply believed in the unity of the universe and that everyone should be able to worship as they pleased. She wanted to go back to visit them, because they were so interesting, but before she got a chance, both men were murdered.

Charles Scudder was proud of his home and loved showing it off to close friends and occasionally locals who visited. There have been many stories of wild homosexual orgies at the guest house or the chicken house on the property, but another visitor, Louis Sizemore, told interviewers he'd been to the house several times and never witnessed anything like that. He said Charles had read *Hamlet* and the stories of Edgar Allan Poe to him. He said Charles was very friendly, but that he didn't see Joey Odom much.[4]

Joseph Odom was, according to friends who knew him, a quiet, "feminine" kind of man who loved to cook and was quite good at it. The two men entertained often and there was even a wedding on the property on one occasion. In 1977, soon after they finished building the home, Joseph Odom, or Joey to his friends, then around thirty-five years old, was badly injured in a car accident on the mountain road leading to the property. The reports were that he was a passenger in a Jeep driven by a friend when the Jeep, going too fast, overturned on the rough, rocky mountain road. He was quite seriously injured and friends say he never regained his full mental capacities after the accident. Scudder spent his time caring for his partner and his medical and pharmaceutical knowledge no doubt came in handy.

"Joey was hurt pretty bad there for a while," Scudder said in the 1979 interview with the Summerville News. "I had to care for him as you would an invalid."

Not much else is known about Joseph Odom. Joey was younger than Scudder by almost twelve years, and was born on March 27, 1938 in Cook County, Illinois. He stopped attending school at the fifth grade, and had been in some minor trouble with the law at some point. He had three sisters, one of whom was Mary L. Odom, the wife of James Isadore Fiumefreddo, of Hopkinsville, Kentucky. Mrs. Fiumefreddo acknowledged her brother's homosexuality.

According to his obituary, Joey "always dreamed of cooking on a woodstove, and wanted to live a simpler life". He unplugged electrical appliances when not in use and kept them "tied in knots, as if to choke them," according to Scudder. On the surface, it would seem that the two men had little in common. Dr. Scudder was quite well educated, and was by all accounts a brilliant man who was the author of several papers and scholarly journals while he taught at Loyola University. Joey had little formal education, yet Dr. Scudder always spoke of him most affectionately and wrote of him in an article for Mother Earth Magazine, "Joseph had learned far more about the world than I had with all my degrees... and somewhere along the line he'd developed a talent for whipping up meals fit for a king!" At the time of the murders, Joey would have been forty-four years old.

By 1970, Scudder's children were mostly grown and Scudder began to want something more out of life. According to an article written on December 19, 1982, and printed in the Chicago Tribune, officials at Loyola University said they had no records of Scudder after 1977 and that "he simply dropped out of sight." Actually, he quit his job at Loyola and moved to Georgia to start a new life.

Friends of Scudder's said he wanted to get out of the hustle and bustle of everyday life and get back to something far simpler. He and Joey Odom mostly grew their own food, for example, after Scudder published a paper in conjunction with his colleague, Dr. Alexander Karczmar, who was the head of the Pharmacology Department at Loyola. The paper linked brain abnormalities to food preservatives. Friends of Scudder's also reported him saying that in the isolated Georgia mountains, he'd be safe from nuclear attacks. This idea would not have been an eccentricity of Scudder's. In the mid-seventies, it was not unusual for the general public to be worried about the cold war with Russia and nuclear attacks.

On December 17, 1975, after several months of searching for land throughout the southeast, Charles Scudder and his long-time companion and partner came to the Summerville, Georgia area. Dr. Scudder bought the south-east quarter of lot 248, 6th Land District of

Chattooga County, Georgia for the sum of $10,500, from John S.
Cooper of Floyd County.[5] It consisted of forty acres of forest land.
Scudder apparently decided in 1976, on his fiftieth birthday, to
resign from LUC and move with his partner, friend, and housekeeper
Joseph Odom to Chattooga County in order to enjoy a simpler
lifestyle in the beautiful mountains of the Chattahoochee National
Forest.

Scudder and Odom built their home from Scudder's own design
on top of their piece of the mountain and named the house and land
Corpsewood Manor, because of the skeletal appearance of the
surrounding trees when Scudder and Odom first arrived on a cold,
snowy winter day in 1976. They lived in a travel trailer while they
built the home, and it took them two years of hard work to build it by
hand.

Sheriff McConnell described the house to the Tribune as "a
medieval, castle-type residence." From the pictures which Scudder
took himself for a magazine article in the Mother Earth Times, he
house appears to be a rather small, fairly ordinary looking two-story
structure made of red brick, with small windows and chimneys on
either end. There are several arches on the structure, including a kind
of small arched portico on the front of the house. A small sculpture
of a pink-painted, concrete gargoyle sits atop the portico. This
gargoyle overlooked a rose garden tended to by Odom. To a person
unfamiliar with gargoyles, its appearance may have been unusual,
even frightening, though gargoyles are not considered to be evil.
They are often used on top of churches, such as at the Notre Dame

Cathedral in Paris, and are said to frighten off and protect those that it guards from any evil or harmful spirits. In addition they were originally used to help in drainage and their elongated frames determine how far water is thrown from the wall.

This is Scudder's account of the move to Georgia and the building of his house in his own words, taken from a magazine article in *Mother Earth* magazine in the March/April edition, 1981. It's important to read it in its entirety to understand more about who Scudder was. While not providing any personal details, the article tell a story of his happiness and tranquility on his own piece of land, made all the more poignant because of what happened to Scudder and Odom just six short years after they purchased it. The article, reprinted here, has a byline of Pamela Purcell and was written by Charles Scudder himself. It tells of the decision to move to Georgia and how they built their dream house.

Corpsewood, circa 1982
The gazebo/sundeck, where tea was served each afternoon on the
front of the house

CORPSEWOOD: THE EYEWITNESS ACCOUNT

Photo Credit: Pamela Purcell, Mother Earth News.

I was "old" when I came into a modest inheritance which amounted to a monthly income of around one hundred dollars. I was pretty much alone, too, with my wife gone and all of my children grown up.

Furthermore, my house was no castle in the country. I lived in an old mansion in a decaying residential area that was more like a mausoleum, a tomb requiring care, cleaning, and endless costly repairs. I was plagued with taxes, light bills, gas bills, water bills, heating bills, and the helpless feeling that resulted from watching my old neighborhood disintegrate into an urban ghetto.

There were other factors prodding me toward a life-changing decision, too. I had a "good job" as an associate professor in a medical school, so I received a salary raise each year, but—of course—it was always more than swallowed up by inflation.

And as time passed, the medical students grew more unruly and less interested in learning. The standards of the school steadily dropped, and my department became a hotbed of "office politics," backbiting, and resentment.

As soon as I got home each evening I'd change into my old (and not too clean or mended) jeans and muddle about in the garden, finding there the only real moments of satisfaction left in my urban life. (I was even pleased when the city's wildlife, the rats, drank from my garden pool at night!)

In such a melancholy environment, it was no wonder that I suffered (along, no doubt, with many others) from continual hankering, vexation, and apathy. But then I inherited my little income, and I thought, "I want out. Oh man! Do I ever want out!"

The only person I really had to consider before making a move was my loyal friend and housekeeper Joe, who—for seventeen years—had cooked for me and my boys and cared for the mansion. He'd been in trouble with the law once and had only a fifth-grade education, but he'd learned far more about the world than I had with all my degrees...and somewhere along the line he'd developed a talent for whipping up meals fit for a king!

It seemed out of the question for me to ask Joe to move to a pretty, ticky-tacky house in the suburbs, because he seemed to have an inherent dislike for anything modern. (He even kept the cords of our few electrical appliances tied in knots, as if to choke them!) My companion also insisted on using iron skillets and old ironstone platters in his kitchen, confessing once that he'd always wanted to cook on a wood stove. Furthermore, I knew I could never live in an apartment, a type of dwelling which I consider to be only slightly better than a prison. So I wondered, "Where shall we go? What shall we do?" And, with my little inheritance providing the necessary impetus for change, I made up my mind. "Why not make a clean break now," I concluded. "Why not get back to basics...be poor!"

After some soul-searching conversations with Joe, I decided that we really needed to find some place in hilly country, with the glamour of four seasons but without super-cold winters, with a good supply of pure water and wood for heating and cooking, and—most important—with a measure of isolation. (After years of enduring the sensory overload of city life, I desperately wanted to be situated where I could neither see nor hear my neighbors.)

I studied geological survey maps of southern states and wrote to the presidents of local realty boards. One such person answered that he had forty inexpensive acres of hardwood trees in the Appalachian foothills, completely surrounded by national forest land. I figured that the cash from the sale of my city property, plus my retirement fund and the money in escrow, would allow me to make such a move, so I drove down to Georgia to take a look. There I found hummingbirds, whippoorwills, butterflies, bobcats, great oaks, fungi, and rolling mountain woodland. I was hooked!

While still lecturing, I bought the land, had a well dug (one hundred and sixty feet deep), planned my house, and bought a little camper and a Jeep.

Then, in 1976—on my fiftieth birthday—I resigned from the school, auctioned off all the furniture and possessions I didn't care about, gave away all my electrical appliances, sold my property, and arranged for a moving company to take charge of the things I wanted to keep. Then Joe and I (plus my two English mastiffs) left for our "kingdom."

Cutting ties that have taken a lifetime to form is a draining experience, and throwing away professional security and all its supposed conveniences and luxuries is like losing a piece of oneself. But for me, the change was like crawling out of an old, outworn skin.

The round outhouse, circa 1982
Photo Credit: Pamela Purcell, Mother Earth News

What an exhilarating, unsettling, and strange rebirth it was!
Joe, the dogs, and I left the city during an icy blizzard. We lost our
way several times in the course of the trip, couldn't find the
property. When we did reach the area, we spent the night parked and
lost. And after we had finally located our new home site, the storm
grew worse. Dead Horse Road (our winding, logging-trail driveway)
disappeared completely.

For the next few days we were alone and stranded in the

wilderness, and had to begin our new life by melting snow for our water supply. In the blizzard-bound quiet we faced up to the incredible amount of work that loomed ahead and the fact that we had much to learn our first task was to list our priorities and to make necessary purchases. The most important buys were a chainsaw, a two-wheeled dolly, a small concrete mixer, a garden cultivator, and a kerosene refrigerator. (We'd already picked up a wood stove at a flea market in the city.) These and all of our other possessions, which the movers eventually brought to the foot of the mountain, were put into temporary storage under plastic sheets weighted down with stones. As we cleared the forest and built—by hand—our house, we celebrated each achievement with a bottle of homemade wine. The following list defines a few of our most memorable days: Relying upon a tripod of logs for a makeshift "derrick," we installed the entire pumping system in the well casing. Our first burst of accomplishment came when free, clean, cold, and delicious mountain water began gushing out of the hand pump. (Water Day!)

After a good bit of experimentation, we set up the kerosene refrigerator and actually got it to work. (Ice Cube Day!)

We dug trenches and installed pipes for sinks, a tile field, and the chemical toilet, which was later enclosed in a round, brick outhouse. (Privy Day?)

Using only hand tools, we dug the excavation for the house's foundation, lined it with bricks, and filled it with concrete and boulders. We used 45,000 bricks to raise the walls of the house...

placing them three layers thick with two-inch-wide air spaces between the layers for insulation. Even so, the cost was quite low and the results pleasing, though I'd never laid a brick before in my life!

A rear view of Corpsewood, circa 1982 Photo Credit: Pamela Purcell, Mother Earth News

By the end of the first summer, we were able to move into the first floor, which contains the kitchen, dining room, and living room. During the second year, we put a roof over our two upstairs bedrooms, which are reached by a circular stairway that's illuminated by my own stained glass window.

And of course, we celebrated Foundation Day, Beam Day, and—at long last—Roof Day!

My message is that we older people are really free—even more so than are young folks—and, because of our experiences, perhaps at least a little more wise. If we want a different, fuller, more exciting life than we're leading—one closer to this beautiful earth— we can have it. Our only chains are those in our minds!

Just promise me that you'll think about it seriously for a while ... after all, wouldn't you like to live in your own kind of "castle in the country?"

--From the article, "Castle In The Country", written by Charles Scudder for Mother Earth News, March/April 1981 edition.

****

From all accounts, Scudder and Odom at first lived a happy, peaceful existence on their land, making good friends in the nearby communities of both Rome and Summerville. People in the area who knew the men and are still living there today talk favorably about them and say they were friendly and never bothered anyone. They had friends who would visit them in their home, but in the seventies and early eighties, in the conservative south, gay men had to be extremely private and circumspect. Friends say they had no quarrel with the local residents and were respected by them. "I loved Charles just like he was a member of my own family," said Mrs. Candie Grogan, in an interview for the news magazine printed after the murders. She was, according to the interview, a friend of the two men who visited them occasionally. "It's beyond me how just by hearsay people can judge one another."

A clerk in the Mountain View Grocery and General Merchandise, Lowanna Stowe, where Scudder and Odom sometimes bought groceries said, "They were nice people. Both were friendly. They were just as nice as they could be when they came in here."[6] Sonny Durham, another friend of the men, said, "They would trust anyone who went up there. We all warned them not to trust everybody."[7]

Greg Hall, another local resident said, "They were friendly to everyone who came around, unless people got nasty with them. Then they would ask them to leave. They just wanted to live their own lives and let others do the same. They were different, but still nice people."[8]

Mrs. Grogan, who admitted she thought Charles Scudder's beliefs were unusual, said, Joey was a Catholic. Charles just worshipped nature. "There's nothing wrong with having books on the occult and witchcraft in your home," she said.[9] Another visitor, a Ms. B. Cooper, said she asked him once about the devil worship, and he said, "No we don't worship the devil. What it really is, is that we think everybody should have the freedom to worship as they choose."

As for the unusual objects in the house, John Mellar a friend from Chicago said, "Those were antiques friends had given him (Scudder) and some of the things, the skulls, the pink gargoyle and the statues were things Charles had collected. They were rare and expensive. He owned a bed that was four hundred years old."[10]

After their move to Georgia, Joseph Odom was involved in the serious automobile that left him in an invalid state for several months, but friends, neighbors and visitors to Corpsewood still knew Odom for his culinary skills.

Scudder said, *"People often fantasize about trying out different (and usually, at least in the imagination, far better) lifestyles, but few actually change the way they live. Social commitments, habit systems, and inertia stop most such dreamers cold. They just don't know that all it takes to realize a fantasy is a small amount of money, a bit of luck, and a whole lot of courage.*

Within two short years we were living in an elegant mini-castle. Our small country estate boasted a circular rose garden at the end of the drive; fruit trees and grapevines; a vegetable garden that produced fresh corn, cabbage, carrots, turnips, and other edibles; and a brick gazebo topped by a sun deck, overlooking the garden, where we take tea. We use many homegrown and foraged food products and our meals must certainly be among the best in the world. After all—as Joe instinctively knew—nothing compares with wood stove cooking!

In fact, we live in a grand style on a little over two hundred dollars a month! Of course, we have no electricity, no phone, and no television set ... but we don't miss those things: We also have no electric bill, no phone bill, no water bill, and no fuel bill. We owe no one!

True, we spend a little on taxes, gasoline, kerosene, and insurance, but most of our meager income goes for food. However, the garden, the fruit trees, and our flock of chickens reduce our grocery needs a bit further each year, and—in time—we expect to produce almost everything we need to eat and more.

This morning, for example, I picked fresh raspberries to go along with our whole wheat pancakes (we grind our own flour from wheat that we buy for $7.00 per 100 pounds!), and honey from our beehives served as syrup. Then I weeded, pumped water, and went about my other chores. At 10:00 a.m., we had tea in the gazebo, and I designed a new chicken-house that I plan to start building soon. Tonight, I may practice my harp. Or perhaps I'll just sit in the courtyard and listen to the tree frogs and whippoorwills, while bats fly and the clouds drift across the full moon. The world that's around me now is fresh, quiet, and very beautiful! The fact is, I'm writing this story simply to give hope to other old rebels like me. It's not necessary, you see, to keep piling up the bucks and plodding away at the treadmill until the last crippling coronary takes away your freedom of choice. There's a time to make a change, and that time is before the rocking chair takes charge of you!

There is, of course, no single simple blueprint for everyone, since personal needs and responsibilities vary. But why be tricked into working the whole year in an uptight world, only to earn a couple of harried "vacation" weeks in an expensive summer cottage? Why enter the "golden years" filled with remorse for things undone?"

--From "Castle In The Country", Mother Earth News, March/April 1981

The spiral staircase leading to the second floor and a glimpse of the
dining room
Photo Credit: Pamela Purcell, Mother Earth News

Sadly, of course, Charles Scudder never got a chance to live his golden years, because a little over a year and a half after the publication of this article, both Charles Scudder and Joseph Odom, along with their two beautiful mastiff dogs, would be murdered in the isolated home they'd built so proudly.

Chapter Three

"The motive for the murders appeared to be "fifty percent the men's lifestyle and fifty percent robbery."
— Sheriff McConnell

Scudder and Odom's Alternative Lifestyle

Photo credit / source: hauntingsingeorgia.blogspot.com

"I love being away from the city," Scudder said in an article for the Summerville News in 1979. "It was a change for the better. I was sick of people and wanted to get back to the basics and myself. I thought it was a rational idea the way the economy was going."

Even though most people in the area liked and admired Charles Scudder and Joseph Odom, accounts of their unconventional lifestyle began to circulate and the two became a subject for gossip and rumor. First of all there was their close relationship and living arrangements. That Scudder and Odom had a serious, long-term romantic relationship cannot be in doubt. Not only were they together for some twenty-three years, but everyone who knew them acknowledged them as a couple.

Dr. Scudder moved Joey into his home in Chicago in 1959, shortly after his estrangement from his wife. He provided for him for the next twenty-three years. He brought Joey with him to Georgia, tenderly cared for him after his accident and left everything to Joey in his will, which reads, in part, "It is my intention by this Will to provide for my good friend Joseph Odom, to the exclusion of all other persons." Any of these facts alone would provide strong circumstantial evidence of a romantic involvement, but taken all together they leave little doubt.

Investigators called the chicken coop Scudder's "pleasure palace," and his "trick room," and said they had a "library of pornographic literature." Scudder himself referred to the third floor of the chicken house, a wooden structure behind his home (hardly a "pleasure palace"), as his guest room. It could, indeed, have been a place he took other men, as there were mattresses on the floor. Or perhaps it was a place he took casual visitors and friends to party, since he didn't like people he didn't know well to come to his house. As for the library, others have indicated he kept stacks of gay magazines, much like heterosexual men of that time often had stacks of old *Playboy* and *Penthouse* magazines in their homes, on the second floor of the wooden structure, a place he used for storage.

Before Scudder and Odom are condemned for their choices, it's important to note that the lifestyles of gay couples were extremely different from that of straight couples in 1982 and remain so even to this day. The same standards of monogamy do not always apply, often by mutual agreement.

Indeed there are a number of stereotypes that were propagated when police investigators and members of the media have given interviews concerning the case. As Murray Lipp, a well-known LGBT activist in New York City states on the website Mic.com, "Myths and stereotypes that go unchallenged become stronger weapons for those who seek to oppress others in society." He feels as if many of these stereotypes are lies. He says, "Myths abound about the apparent promiscuity of gay men as though sex with multiple partners and an inability to be monogamous are core features of male homosexuality–they aren't. Sexual promiscuity, when it occurs, is a human phenomenon that is not uniquely linked with one particular type of sexual orientation. As with any group of people, the sexual behavior of gay men varies tremendously from person to person, with some being very sexually active and others being almost completely celibate. In common with all human beings, gay men have sexual desire. The suggestion by opponents of equality that male homosexual desire is inherently more 'sexual' or more 'hedonistic' than heterosexual desire is ludicrous."

However, there is dissension about this fact even within the LGBT community. Other bloggers like Robert Lindsay, an LGBT blogger on his blog site "Beyond Highbrow" says, "Gay men have always been insanely promiscuous. This has been a feature of gay male culture in the US for much of this century. There is nothing new about it. It exploded in the 1970s as new opportunities arose for gay men to have many more partners than before. The promiscuity leveled off somewhat in the 1980s and since, but it is still quite common for gay men to have many, many more sexual partners than the average straight man does. Truth is that straight men are probably not that much different than gay men. If there were enough women out there so that having sex with fifty to three hundred women a year was not nearly impossible, I am quite certain that a lot of straight men would do just that."

Charles Scudder has also been accused of being promiscuous, but even the word "promiscuous" has a negative connotation, as if they're doing something wrong, which may not be the case. Then as now, homosexual relationships may certainly be as loving and stable as heterosexual relationships. In fact, most lesbians are very monogamous. But it's perhaps difficult for heterosexuals to understand that particularly in the seventies or early eighties, not all gay couples expected or even necessarily wanted monogamy. Some couples who were long-term often were able to be that way simply because they didn't practice monogamy by the consent of both parties. This was certainly not true of all gay relationships, by any means. It is simply to say that it was not unheard of in the community to not be monogamous then or even now.

This is in no way to imply that heterosexual relationships are "better" or that homosexual relationships are worse on some societal moral scale. They're just different, and gay men, particularly in the late seventies and early eighties, before AIDS became so widespread, were often very sexually active, much more so than straight men.

In fact, many gays in the seventies turned their backs on what they thought of as "heterosexual" morality and standards of behavior, just as they believed heterosexual society had already turned its back on them. Gay men often had their own culture and their own belief system. It's possible and even likely that Scudder and Odom, though they may have been, according to all accounts, in a stable and loving relationship, did not always practice monogamy.

It's difficult for us from a perspective in 2015 to know or realize how repressive society was to gays in the 1970s and '80s. A number of U.S. states repealed sexually restrictive laws during this decade— laws that had criminalized same-sex behavior as misdemeanors or felonies. These laws were called by various names: anti-sodomy, unnatural intercourse, crimes against nature, sexual misconduct, etc. Considering the profound stigma which as still attached to homosexuality at the dawn of the 1970s, gay rights saw huge gains over the course of the decade, but most men in 1982, especially older men like Scudder, still had to be careful to keep their secrets. Perhaps this was one of the reasons Scudder decided to move to such an isolated area and refused to allow visitors to come inside his home. He would have been frightened to do so, and with good cause. Unfortunately, Scudder may not have been careful enough.

The two men were not open to everyone about their arrangement. Perhaps their friends knew, but this was 1982. Gay men didn't always share their status openly, especially in rural Georgia. Still, the word got around pretty quickly, and most everyone knew of their relationship.

For a small, conservative area like Trion, people were surprisingly tolerant, and though they didn't necessarily approve, they didn't seem to give them many problems about it. The two men kept to themselves, according to all reports.

Not everyone in the area was so tolerant and open-minded. Sheriff McConnell, in his interview with the *Chicago Tribune*, when asked to describe the relationship between Scudder and Odom, said, "Odom was Scudder's servant, his lackey, his boy." He went on to say, "They [Scudder and Odom] were involved in homosexual activity and devil worship."

Undoubtedly, Scudder and Odom were involved in homosexual activity, as are approximately four percent of the world's population, according to most polls. But what about the charges of devil worship? Can these charges finally be laid to rest? It remains a source of gossip and frequent references to Corpsewood as "the devil-worshippers' house" seem to resist any attempt to prove them false. This is how their murderers referred to Corpsewood, and is the one charge that continues to be leveled at them and doesn't ever seem to go away.

From close to the beginning of the time they lived in Chattooga County, there were rumors about devil worship. At one time the rumors got so bad Gary McConnell tried to bring charges against Dr. Scudder and Joseph Odom, as stated earlier, but was unable to have them arrested because of their beliefs. The sheriff was reminded of the freedom of religion laws, but perhaps the damage had already been done. Wild stories persist to this day.

When the authors went to the site they were stopped at one point on the isolated dirt road leading to the property and asked for directions by woman in a van. After speaking with her for a few minutes, she asked them where they were going. They replied, "To Corpsewood," and she said, "Oh, that devil worshippers' house." This is how nearly everyone in the community still refers to it, even after nearly thirty-three years have passed. The accusation has to be examined in detail because of its importance to the case.

Everyone, from investigators down to the murderers themselves has used this, perhaps unconsciously, as a way to blame the victims for what happened to them. In an interview for a news magazine about the case, Tony Gilliland, chief investigator for the Chattooga County Sheriff's Office said, "There is no argument, I am sure, that their lifestyle was strange—unacceptable to most of us." Speaking of the house itself, he said, "There was a spirit present. Of that I am convinced. A spirit of evil. It made the skin prickle and beads of perspiration pop out on the forehead in the cold mountain temperature…the odor. What was it? A breath of the nether world? It was…the very lifestyle of the victims."

Pretty colorful language for a police investigator and it points out the circus-like atmosphere, along with the hyperbole used by law enforcement in the days following the murder.

Sheriff McConnell told the *Tribune* the men's home was "adorned with skulls, satanic altars, and bizarre sexual instruments." He said the scene was like something "out of a horror movie," with "skulls scattered all over the house." F.B.I. agent Brad Bonnell, quoted in the same article, even speculated on the murderers' incentives for the shooting. He said, "The killers may have been inspired by a grisly painting found upstairs in the home of a gagged man with blood dripping from five bullet holes in his forehead. That's about how Scudder looked when we found him."

It's difficult to imagine an F.B.I. agent making such a statement today, but such was the carnival atmosphere in the days following the murders. When describing Scudder and Odom's two mastiff dogs, also found shot to death by the wood stove, McConnell said they were "as big as Shetland ponies." He said he considered the motive for the murders to be "fifty percent the men's lifestyle and fifty percent robbery." [11]

Seven pastors from the local churches were given a tour of Corpsewood on December 16, 1982, only four days after the murders. Today it would be unheard of to allow so many unrelated sightseers to trample all over the crime scene, and for what purpose? Yet, this visit had to have been allowed by law enforcement. Pastor Jimmy Bryant of the South Summerville Baptist Church told reporters he was "appalled" by what he saw inside Corpsewood. Reverend Jimmy Arthur of Faith Baptist Church said the "filth" at Corpsewood was "unbearable."[12]

****

Were the two men actually devil-worshippers? Were there satanic altars in the house? Unseen "satanic forces" at work? What is the evidence?

Other than some candelabras found in the home, and a few skulls and statues of demonic-looking figures, there seem to have been no "altars" of any kind. Charles Scudder was a professed atheist, so he would have had no need for any place to worship Satan or anyone else.

Friends say Charles Scudder had an intellectual curiosity about the Satanic Church, but was it more than just curiosity? What would make an intelligent, some say brilliant, man like Scudder turn to a study of the Satanic Church?

First of all, it should be made clear that most of that speculation circles around Charles Scudder, and Scudder alone. Joey Odom was, according to his sister, a Roman Catholic. He may not have attended services, but there is no record of his ever joining the Satanic Church. There is also no record of what he actually believed.

Scudder was an atheist, but it's hard to pinpoint how long he might have held those views. To some people in a Christian community like Summerville, being an atheist is almost as bad as worshipping the devil. However, it is also a fact that Scudder worked for many years for Loyola University, a Catholic school, owned and operated by the Jesuits. While the Jesuits might be fairly liberal and encourage cultural diversity at their university, it's to be assumed they would *not* have allowed one of their professors to openly worship Satan.

There is some evidence that Scudder may have been Catholic, or at least he might have been at one time—his long-time employment by a Catholic University, for example. The university does not make religion a term of employment, but the possibility does suggest itself.

Scudder left no record of why he first got involved with or wrote to Anton La Vey, the infamous High Priest of the Satanic Church. Some friends have said Scudder was never really a member, but just curious about it. Scudder and Odom's neighbor, Raymond Williams, told reporters that, "Charles had joined the Satan church (sic) but he said he wasn't a participant. Charles told me he was actually an atheist and that he just joined up to see what it was all about."[13]

Anton LaVey, who was reportedly "enraged and grieved by the injustice of what happened to Scudder and Odom."

Dr. Scudder's membership in the Church of Satan has since been confirmed by Magus Peter H. Gilmore and Magistra Blanche Barton, both of the Church of Satan. However, it's actually more accurate to say he was an *inactive member*, according to the church records, and it's important to know exactly what the church of Satan is before drawing any further conclusions.

Despite the deliberately provocative name, the Satanic Church's high priest, Peter Gilmore, describes its members as "skeptical atheists," and says that the Hebrew root of the word "Satan" means "opposer" or "one who questions."

Most people are not aware that the philosophy of the Church of Satan is in fact atheistic, and its members do not worship any supernatural being. To be as clear as possible, *members of the original Satanic Church, and the one Charles Scudder was in contact with, do not worship Satan.*

This is not to say that some individuals may practice so-called devil worship—but Gilmore rejects these people. He says those who call themselves Satanists and say they believe Satan to be a supernatural being or force that may be contacted or supplicated to are the true "devil worshipers," *not his church.* Gilmore says, "My real feelings are that anybody who believes in supernatural entities on some level is insane. Whether they believe in the Devil or God, they are abdicating reason." [14]

Gilmore went on to add "Satanism begins with atheism. We begin with the universe and say, 'It's indifferent. There's no God, and there's no Devil. No one cares!'"[15]

The founder of the Church, Anton Szandor LaVey, said that he had been in communication with Dr. Scudder, and had visited Corpsewood (the date of his visit is unknown and was possibly after Scudder and Odom's murders), but there is no proof of his visit. According to Barton, "Dr. LaVey was enraged and grieved by the injustice of what happened to them." LaVey viewed the murders as evidence that there were still areas in the United States where eccentrics were still attacked for holding beliefs outside of the norm. A few weeks before his murder, Scudder had received a birthday card from San Francisco from the Church of Satan that wished him a happy fifty-sixth birthday.

So then, even if Scudder was a participating member of the church, and from what his friends say, he was not, there was no "devil-worshipping" aspect to his membership. Scudder was an atheist. Bad enough in the conservative, Christian south, but still a long way away from actually worshipping a satanic being. Thus there would be no need for 'satanic altars" as Sheriff McConnell called them, and there was no evidence of them in the crime scene photographs taken in the home.

As rumors of "Satan worship" grew, so did the occasional drunken visits by truckloads of the curious, who wanted to "burn the devil worshippers out." Charles Scudder would go out to meet them and talk to them in a friendly manner, turning them away. One friend said he "could talk you into anything, or out of it." No one ever stayed to do harm. Perhaps that lulled Scudder into a false sense of security, thinking he could handle any ill-wishers on his own. Still, for a man who had given up his home in Chicago and come to the mountains looking for peace and tranquility and the chance to live the life he chose for himself, these invasions of his privacy must have been burdensome and exhausting.

The men owned two large mastiff dogs, but the dogs didn't seem to present any real threat to visitors. One of the dogs was named Beelzebub, was larger than the other, though not as large as any kind of pony. A grown mastiff can weigh as much as one hundred and sixty pounds and can stand as tall as thirty-six inches. In truth, there is no evidence that either of the dogs was vicious at all. On the night they were killed, they were shot as they lay peacefully by a wood stove. Mastiffs are not usually attack animals. In fact, despite their large size, the English Mastiff is a very peaceful and tolerant breed. Even if another dog attacks it, the Mastiff will often turn his back on the opponent. He won't fight unless he has to. Self-defense is the only reason for an average Mastiff to use his strength.

Charles Scudder and Beelzebub
Photo Credit: Find a Grave website

What of Scudder's will and his relationship or lack of relationship with his family? There is quite a bit of evidence to suggest Dr. Scudder was estranged from his family. He never divorced his wife, yet told people his former wife was dead when she was not. He made a will leaving everything to Joey Odom and specifically naming and then cutting out his grown sons. After he died, his ashes were not taken by his children nor by his former spouse, but by a sister, and then only after several months. His ashes were not interred until April of 1983.

What can be made of these facts? Could Charles Scudder's estrangement from his family be because he was gay and living openly with Joey Odom?

It is important to remember that the LGBT community has long had and continues to have a complicated relationship with the Christian Church as well as with family members. There are countless stories in the media of parents and families rejecting their loved ones when they "come out" and there are homeless shelters all over the United States that house young men and women whose parents have kicked them out of their homes, sometimes on the advice of their ministers.

The world's major religions vary a great deal. But most denominations are generally negative towards an LGBT orientation. There are many different types of actions churches suggest for dealing with homosexuals, ranging from quietly discouraging homosexual activity to explicitly forbidding same-sex sexual practices and actively opposing social acceptance of the lifestyle. In some countries being gay can lead to imprisonment and even death. Some ministers "hate the sin, but love the sinner" and preach this to their congregations, but others take a harder stance.

The Christian church, then, and notably, the Catholic Church, is not usually accepting of the gay lifestyle, and in some cases, may turn its back on the LGBT community. Is this, perhaps, why Scudder began to practice atheism? Many casual visitors to Corpsewood around this time reported that when asked if they might go inside his home to look around, Scudder replied, "Nobody goes in the professor's house." It's not difficult to surmise why he took that stance. The home he and Joey built by hand was their sanctuary, their dream home. In addition, Charles Scudder was a collector of occult books and objects, and had been for years. A great deal has been made of the occult objects in his home, and again, these objects are used to blame the victims. Yet consider how many television programs currently explore "paranormal activity." An interest in the paranormal certainly doesn't mean that a person is evil.

These were two gay men, with books and magazines inside the home that the investigators after their deaths labeled their "pornographic library." It's little wonder that with a number of drunken locals saying they wanted to burn him out, he was well-advised to keep visitors limited to only close friends and like-minded acquaintances. The vast majority of people who lived in Chattooga County and who visited or knew Scudder and Odom were good people with no harmful intentions. However, it only took two people to destroy Charles Scudder and Joseph Odom and bring their lives and their home to the ruin it is today.

Scudder called his home his "castle in the woods." But Scudder learned that it was a mistake to be too friendly and open about his lifestyle and that it was past time for him to pull up the gates and bar the castle doors. Perhaps that knowledge was too little, too late.

Chapter Four

The Scene of the Crime

On Taylor's Ridge near Corpsewood

Corpsewood Manor was a forty-four foot by sixteen foot brick structure with small masonic type windows, allowing little light into the home. It was two stories and had five rooms, including a library, a kitchen and dining area, two upstairs bedrooms and a hallway. An interior spiral staircase made of stone connected the lower level with the upper floors, and the stairwell contained a stained glass window made by Scudder himself. Only the ruins remain today, almost covered in equal measure by ivy and graffiti.

Still, it's beautiful and even peaceful. The front portico remains intact, though covered with ivy and difficult to navigate through. A few pieces of wall still stand, along with the two rounded structures at the back with arched doorways. There is a makeshift firepit in what might have once been the back courtyard, and a trail at the back leads down to the muscadine vines and the road. It's very quiet there in the woods and we tried to imagine how Charles must have loved the place as he sat out at the back of the house to "listen to the tree frogs and whippoorwills, while bats fly and the clouds drift across the full moon."

The original home had no electricity and was lit by kerosene lamps, so there are no power poles to mar the scenery. The refrigerator was powered by kerosene as well. There was no running water and wood was used for cooking and for heat. A small pond was located just down the hill from the front of the house. The two men lived comfortably on about two hundred dollars a month, an income from the interest on a joint forty-thousand-dollar savings account at a local bank, along with a small inheritance of Scudder's.

The small, dark rooms were furnished with a collection of antiques, brought from Scudder's home in Chicago. He had a bed from the Italian Renaissance Era, dating back to the 1500s, as well as a gold-plated harp that he had learned to play himself without formal training. Scudder's strange collections and antiques—candelabras, gold-plated daggers and occult paraphernalia including skulls and pink painted statues of gargoyles—all painted a false image of wealth, which members of the town would often discuss and speculate on. Items recovered from the manor following the murders only fueled this belief.

According to an agent with the Georgia Bureau of Investigation, two human skulls were discovered, and sent off to the crime lab. Also discovered were, in the words of the F.B.I. report, "miscellaneous items of witchcraft, cult paraphernalia, black candles, etc." The headboard of the master bedroom featured a "devil-like statue," and the house was "riddled with homosexual pornography." (A visitor to the site in the days following the murders said there were some gay magazines scattered around).

A friend of Scudder's said that much of the eccentric "collection" Scudder obtained from a theater in Chicago which was going out of business and selling off all its props. It seems clear that Scudder amused himself with statues of devils and a horned man with fangs, and skulls used as candelabras. There were even two stained glass windows picturing a human skull and a wolf's skull that Scudder designed and made himself. Does this prove that Scudder was a "devil worshipper" or simply a man indulging his eccentric tastes in the privacy of his own home?

In the rear of Corpsewood was a second story verandah, and the couple was planning to build a two-hundred-foot circular pond, surrounded by a natural stone patio. A chemical toilet was situated in an outbuilding along with another outbuilding containing a well. On the grounds were vineyards of muscadines and a garden, where they grew most of their food. They cultivated the muscadines and made their own wine.

The house had chimneys which bore either a pentacle or a pentagram design. The reports are conflicting. Pentacles and pentagrams are considered to be two of the most powerful symbols within the world of occultism and witchcraft. They can be also seen throughout our modern society, being used as earrings, necklaces, on posters, banners, and certain magazine and CD album covers. They can be seen in New Age bookstores and in the occult sections of major book retailers such as Barnes and Noble. They're seen on t-shirts, organizational letterheads, brochures, billboard advertisements, tombstones, and within movies and television shows. Pentacles and pentagrams can obviously be found all over, but what do they mean?

The physical differences between the pentacle and pentagram are minimal. Pentacles are upright five-pointed stars within a circle, while pentagrams often have the point facing down. Within the occult, they supposedly have opposite spiritual properties. From a Christian viewpoint, however, both symbols represent forces that oppose Biblical truth.

From an occult perspective, pentacles are representative of "white" magic and "good." They also represent man's intellect and reason. Oftentimes pentacles are used as a talisman—an inanimate object laced with psychic powers. Used by high-ranking Freemasons and the Eastern Star, the pentacle represents protection. Its purpose was to help gain knowledge of future events, to have power over devils and angels and to do miracles.

There were both pentacles and pentagrams at Corpsewood. Pictures of the stained glass window in Corpsewood show a pentagram, as has been reported. Other symbols, like the one on the side of Scudder's Jeep, seem to be pentacles. The pink gargoyle on Scudder's house may have been intended as a form of protection as well. In light of what eventually happened in that house, it does seem a bit prophetic and also very sad for so many symbols of protection to have been used there.

Also on the grounds of Corpsewood was a three-story, fifty-foot high building called "the chicken coop." The first floor held chickens, the second, storage for canned goods and a store of homosexual literature. The third floor, which was painted pink, was what law enforcement agents called "A guest room and trick chamber."[16] The night of the murders, there was nothing inside the room except for two mattresses on the floor.

The structure was burned to the ground on January 5, 1983, less than a month after the murders, by persons unknown and in mysterious circumstances.

CORPSEWOOD: THE EYEWITNESS ACCOUNT

****

Corpsewood aficionados refer a great deal to a "prophetic" and eerie painting that hung in the home and was reported to have been done by Charles Scudder before the murders. The painting is a morbid subject—a gagged man with eyes, some say, that look like those of a corpse, and five bullet holes in his head. It's a common misconception that when Scudder was found he had five bullet wounds in his head, but this is *not true*, even though a newspaper supplement entitled *Murder at Corpsewood* and published shortly after the crimes erroneously reported it to be so. This supplemental magazine reported several other wildly speculative comments that were unfounded and defamatory to the two victims.

In actual fact, Charles Scudder actually had only four bullet wounds in his body. According to testimonies given by Dr. James Dawson, the Assistant Director of the Georgia Crime Laboratory, who performed the autopsies on the bodies of Scudder and Odom, there were *four* gunshot wounds and Dawson said he removed four .22 caliber bullets from his head. All four bullets were from a rifle. Joey Odom had five bullet wounds, but not in his forehead. All five wounds were behind the left ear.

Painting of gagged man with bullet holes

The man in the portrait doesn't look like Scudder, who was older and had blond hair—the man in the portrait appears to have dark hair and eyebrows. Three different friends of Scudder's said that it was Joey Odom who "dreamed the portrait up." They said it was after his accident and Charles Scudder painted it after he told

67

him about it. None of the friends knew who the man in the portrait was supposed to be. One friend said, "If it was Joey, why wasn't he wearing his glasses?" Also, neither Scudder nor Odom were bound and gagged at the time of their deaths. (Scudder was bound with strips from a sheet when he was taken down to the house, but at the time he was found, the bindings had already been removed). Odom was never bound or gagged.

Tracy Wilson, a Chattooga county woman who visited Scudder frequently alleges that when asked about the painting, Scudder would say, "That's how I'm going to die."

"He told me he saw how he was going to die in a vision," she reported. "He said he had a demon following him around." Mrs. Wilson made several other statements like this in interviews after the murders. However, three other friends of Scudder's dispute her comments, saying the portrait was *not* a self-portrait.[17]

After a visit approximately a month before Scudder was murdered, Mrs. Wilson also said "Charles seemed tense and nervous, like he knew something was going to happen. He worried if Joey could get along without him. It spooked me. He started talking about reincarnation and said he was coming back after death….He knew what you were going to say before you said it."

Tracy Wilson later would give some other testimony of a sensational nature at the trial of Tony West, and has occasionally continued to give such testimony in interviews since that time. West's attorneys were trying to make a case that "there were strange things going on at that house," and that the wine Tony West drank that night was laced with LSD. During the trial, Dr. Scudder was accused of spiking the wine with LSD in order to try to have oral sex with the two men. West tried to use a defense of involuntary intoxication. The defense attorney went as far to say on the matter of the supposed drugging, "He had a motive because he was a homosexual." The jury ignored this prejudicial line of reasoning.[18]

Ms. Wilson said, during her testimony, that she had seen drugs at Corpsewood on occasion, like cocaine. She also said that she had suffered bizarre effects after drinking Scudder's homemade wine, which from all accounts was a very potent brew. She said she had once drunk only a half-cup of wine in the pink room and woke up hours later on top of the ridge, a half mile from the house with no memory of how she got there.

Many of these statements made by the defense and Mrs. Wilson should be considered carefully. The defense teams of Tony West and Avery Brock theorized that the wine was laced with LSD, and pointed to some vials of LSD found in Scudder's desk drawer. They said Dr. Scudder had once been involved in scientific studies of the substance in his lab at Loyola. The bottles of wine drunk by the group on December 12th were examined by the Georgia State Crime Lab and showed absolutely no residue of any drugs. The bottle of wine did not have any trace of LSD and was simply a bottle of muscadine wine. However, due to a technicality, the Crime Lab results were not introduced as evidence at the trials. According to testimony by former colleagues of Scudder, the professor never participated in any LSD experiments even though the batch of LSD-

25 found in Scudder's home was like that used by the CIA in the early eighties for their MK-Ultra experiments.

The question remains—could Scudder, or more accurately, Joey Odom, have had a premonition of his own death as evidenced by the painting? The subject matter of the painting is certainly eerie and the fact that the subject in the painting has five bullet wounds in the head is chilling in light of Joey Odom and Charles Scudder's wounds. If it was some kind of premonition that Joey "dreamed up," then it would have had to have been some kind of composite or amalgamation of what happened to the two men. Could the painting have been just a coincidence? Or was it another wild rumor put forward by those wishing to sensationalize the tragedy? We present it here because of the great interest in the subject, but it would be a matter of purest speculation to say what the painting represents. However, that certainly hasn't stopped anyone from trying.

Chapter Five

"All I can say is that they were devils and I'm glad I killed them."

The Murderers: Tony West and Avery Brock

AVERY BROCK   TONY WEST

Perhaps equally as important as the victims of the crime are the two murderers, though not a great deal is known about the lives of Kenneth Avery Lowrance Brock and Samuel Tony West before the murders at Corpsewood.

In November of 1982, seventeen-year old occasional pulpwood truck driver Avery Brock moved into the rundown Halls Valley trailer of a thirty-year-old unemployed construction worker by the name of Tony West. The mobile home was on a lot blocked by downed trees from the paved road. West told friends he wanted it that way because he didn't want people to bother him. It had no electricity or running water and was situated on land owned by Tony's sister, Myra Haygood, in Walker County, Georgia. Myra was the mother of Joey Wells, who would later be an eyewitness to West's crimes.

Born in 1965, Avery Brock was seventeen years old, about six feet tall, with light brown or sandy-colored hair. He no longer attended school and had no full-time job. He liked to hunt and since the trailer where he lived was only a few miles from the land owned by Dr. Scudder, he sometimes went hunting in that area. That was how he came to meet Charles Scudder and Joseph Odom. He was out hunting one day and came upon Corpsewood and the two men. They were friendly and welcoming, as friends have said they always were, and they struck up a conversation.

After that, Avery made seven or eight more trips into the woods to visit Corpsewood, during which, according to his testimony, he had sexual encounters with Scudder. Brock spent many occasions drinking Scudder's homemade wine in the chicken coop. Their relationship escalated, according to Brock, and he may have been intimately involved with the men on numerous occasions. He told investigators that Charles Scudder "sucked his dick." Friends of Scudder speculate that Brock attempted to initiate a threesome with the couple but was denied.

He told Tony West about the couple and said they appeared to be wealthy and "lived like kings." It was West, according to what Brock told investigators, who came up with the plan to rob the men. Avery Brock told Tony West that the two men appeared to have no friends or relatives in the area, and no one would miss them.

Tony West was born in 1952, in Indiana and moved to Chattanooga, Tennessee, with his mother and sisters soon after his father was killed in a train accident when he was nine years old. When he was fourteen, he was playing with a friend's .22 caliber pistol and accidentally shot his two-year-old nephew in the head, killing him instantly. According to his family, West thought he'd unloaded the gun and pointed it at the infant "to show him there was nothing to fear." He pulled the trigger, sending the bullet into the baby's brain, killing him instantly.[19] The baby's mother, who stood by while he pointed the gun at her child, presumably, and saw the whole thing happen right in front of her.

As West got older, he quit school and was married by the time he was seventeen. He and his wife had five sons. Supposedly, according to family members, he had another illegitimate son by a previous relationship. He worked odd construction jobs for a while, but began having run-ins with the law during the early years of the marriage. In 1978, he was caught stealing tires from a Jeep, found guilty of larceny and sent to a county workhouse.

He wasn't incarcerated long before escaping and while out, he got into an argument with his brother-in-law over a poker game, which culminated in West shooting him. The man was not killed, but the incident resulted in West being charged with aggravated assault and being sentenced to three years in the Pikeville, Tennessee Maximum Security Prison. After serving eighteen months of his sentence, he was released and went home to discover that his wife had left him and his five children had become wards of the state.

During the next few years, West was treated three times in local Chattanooga area mental facilities before moving into the old trailer on his sister's property in Walker County, Georgia. In November, 1982, Tony West met Avery Brock and struck up a fast friendship, resulting in Brock moving in with West that same month.

It couldn't have been long before Avery Brock told West about the "queer devil-worshipers" living in the isolated countryside. Seventeen-year-old Brock's stories must have convinced Tony West they could become wealthy beyond their wildest dreams because of valuables inside the house. Living as the two men did, in an old trailer with no power and no water, the professor's house must have looked like a palace to them.

Tony West said that Avery Brock told him he'd had oral sex with Dr. Scudder on several occasions. Avery Brock also admitted to having visited the men at Corpsewood and he had sex with at least one of the men, according to Tony West's testimony and his own admission. He claimed he was forced to have oral sex, but could that be a misrepresentation of the facts?

Avery Brock was seventeen years old, six feet tall and a healthy young male at the time of the killings. Scudder was in his fifties and only five feet six inches tall. By all accounts and judging from his photographs, he was a slight figure, not overly muscular or strong. It seems unlikely that anything was "forced" if it did indeed occur. Could Avery Brock have been "seduced" by a much older and more experienced man? Perhaps, and yet Brock was obviously not so traumatized that it prevented him from returning again and again to the home in the woods in the days before the murders.

Scudder and Odom's relaxed demeanor and effortless existence may have given Brock the false impression that Scudder and Odom had stockpiled an immense fortune and all he and West had to do was take it for themselves. In a small town where rumors and gossip became gospel, Brock and West convinced themselves it would be easy for them to waltz in and take what they wanted. The fact that Charles Scudder refused to allow Avery to enter his home further fueled the idea that the two men kept a treasure inside the home. Whenever Avery Brock visited, Dr. Scudder entertained him in the chicken coop, as he called it, a fifty-foot-high wooden structure behind the home. The bottom part housed chickens. The second floor was used for storage and the third was where Scudder took visitors to drink wine and possibly indulge in sexual activities, should they be so inclined.

During the trial of Tony West, Dr. Scudder was accused of spiking the wine with LSD in order to try to have oral sex with both men. Teresa Hudgins said she saw no sign of this the night of the killings. All they did before the violence started was sit around and talk and pass around a bottle of wine. She distinctly remembers the bottle being passed to her, and she put the bottle to her mouth but passed it along, not being used to drinking and not liking the taste.

She suffered no LSD-like effects but neither did she observe any in the other men, including Joey Wells, who stated to investigators that he had drunk the wine.

Disillusioned by their lives, and seeing no way out unless they took what they needed from others, Brock and West confessed to investigators that they hatched a plot to rob the Scudder and Odom of their fortune and run away. Tony West and Avery Brock decided that once they had Scudder and Odom's fortune, they would be free to live their lives as they had always dreamed.

After hatching the burglary plan with West, Brock's visits took on new meaning. In November of 1982, he visited what he called the "castle in the woods" several times in an attempt to study the layout of the house. Unfortunately, his sexual encounters with Scudder continued to be limited to the Pink Room, and he was never granted entry into Corpsewood Manor.

The wheels were set in motion, however, and the plan was set. Less than a month after moving in together, Tony West and Avery Brock would commit senseless and heinous crimes together and murder three men in cold blood. In addition, during interviews by the authorities, accusations flew back and forth between the two killers, each one accusing the other of being the primary shooter. One of the men, Avery Brock, even tried to implicate the eyewitness Joey Wells, the nephew of Tony West, to the crime. The killers claimed they were drugged by the victims and their defense teams used their allegations and stories to try to explain the horrific nature of their crimes.

Chapter Six

"I asked for this."

The Murders of Charles Scudder and Joseph Odom

From the first time Teresa told us this story, we were hooked. Not only because of the truly chilling eyewitness account, nor because the murder and trial drew international attention in its day, but also because of the tragic fate of the two victims, who continue to this day to be vilified by some as "devil worshippers."

Rather than sift through the accounts of what happened as told by the two murderers, we chose instead to tell the story of the night of the murder the way we heard it first, exactly as Teresa told us.

After reading transcripts from the trial, numerous interviews of the principal parties by law enforcement and countless blogs, websites, and magazine articles all telling slightly different stories, we wanted to tell the story of the eyewitness to the crime. The only person who was not either directly involved in the murders or related to the murderers—and that person is Teresa Hudgins.

These are Teresa's memories after thirty years have passed. It was a traumatic, horrible event. She continues to have nightmares about it till this day. However, we believe that her story is truly the most authentic because she was there. She lived it. And she survived

78

that terrible night.

Over the years, she has told us many people in the area have wondered why the "eyewitness" hasn't stepped forward on social media sites to tell what she knows. She's stepping forward now, and this is her exclusive story.

In December of 1982, my daughter and I were staying with a friend and his family. I was eighteen years old and my little girl was two. I don't remember now how exactly how long we'd been staying there. I'd left my husband some time before after catching him with another woman, and I was hurt and disappointed, because once again my hope of having a happy family life was gone.

I remember that I thought Joey Wells was a nice-looking boy, and I wanted to go out with him when he asked me. His mother, Myra Hopgood, came to pick me up at the friend's house and I left my daughter with them, telling them I was going to play Bingo. My plan was to be gone for a couple of hours and then go home to my daughter. I loved her very much—she was all I had, and I was a good mother.

When I got there, Joey told me that he was having car trouble and that we were going to go riding around with his uncle, Tony West and the man I later found out was his roommate, Avery Brock. Tony was Myra's brother, and he lived in a trailer on some land that his sister owned in Walker County, Georgia. Walker County and Chattooga County, where the murders took place, are adjacent to each other.

I felt uneasy and nervous as Joey and I climbed into the backseat of Tony's red Plymouth Javelin. Even more so when I saw the .22 caliber rifle between the two front seats. I was uncomfortable and tried to make a little joke, asking if they planned to kill me. Avery said that they carried the gun with them in case they needed it. I knew that Avery liked to hunt, and since every time I saw Avery he had a gun or an axe or something to kill animals with, I didn't think all that much about it. I just accepted what they said about it, but there was that gut feeling that I shouldn't go with them that night. I wish to God I had paid attention to that feeling and that little voice inside me.

I had no idea we were going up to Corpsewood until we were already in the car. In fact, I didn't know what Corpsewood even was. I sat next to Joey in the car and I think we held hands. I remember we stopped at a store on the way to buy cigarettes, Marlboro Reds, and we got a dollar's worth of gas.

I said to Joey, "Why did you just buy a dollar's worth? That won't get us far."

And he said, "We're going up to the devil-worshippers' house and drink some free homemade wine."

I didn't even drink back then and I had no desire to go. I said, "Devil Worshippers? What are they?"

And Avery spoke up from the front seat and said, "Just queer men. They won't hurt you."

I was still nervous, but I went along with it, hoping for the best.

The first thing I remember after we got up to Taylor's Ridge and found the road was the sign on the way to the house. "Beware the Thing." I asked about it and Joey told me not to worry about it. He said it was just to keep people away.

I was still feeling uneasy as we pulled into the yard. Tony blew the horn and Charles Scudder, a short blond man, came out of the house and over to the car. He asked, "You guys got a cigarette?" He explained that Joey (Odom), his companion, would probably like to have one. They gave it to him and asked if we could get out. He said that we could and that we'd all go up to the guest house. I later learned that this was also called the pink room or the chicken coop. I said, "Why can't we just go in the house?"

Mr. Scudder said, "Nobody goes in the professor's house."

I thought that was odd, but I went with the other men to a building where we climbed a ladder to the third floor. We came up into a pink room with two mattresses on the floor. Joey and I sat down on one of them. Scudder left, saying he'd go get some wine. Tony and Avery sat on the other mattress. Nobody said much, only making what seemed like to me to be general small talk.

When Mr. Scudder returned, he brought with him three or four bottles of red wine, but I don't remember Mr. Scudder drinking any of it. They passed the bottle to me at one point, and I put it to my lips but took it right back down again. I wasn't a drinker and I didn't like the taste or the smell. They kept talking and I really didn't pay much attention about what. I was holding Joey's hand at this point. I never drank any more wine, though Joey drank some. Avery said he was

81

going downstairs to get something out of his car and when he came back he had the .22 rifle.

In the trial and on a lot of the websites people say that we were sniffing toot-a-loo on the way up to Corpsewood in the car. Avery said at the trial that he went down to the car to get some more of it, but I don't remember him ever saying that. We definitely were not doing that on the way up the mountain, no matter what they said later. I had never heard of toot-a-loo and wouldn't have known what it was anyway. I didn't do drugs. They must have had some in their car that I didn't see, but nobody was doing that on the drive up there or at any time before or after we left Joey's house. I think they just said all that to try to make people think they were too intoxicated to know what they were doing.

Author's Note: "toot-a-loo," a mixture of varnish, paint thinner, and other things in a plastic bag is sniffed to get high.

Avery sat the rifle down, and Mr. Scudder laughed and said, "Bang, bang." Then the next thing I remember is Mr. Scudder standing up to adjust an oil lamp. Avery pulled a knife from his boot, jumped up and grabbed Mr. Scudder by his hair. He held the knife to his throat. He told him he wanted money and Mr. Scudder said he didn't have any. Tony started cutting up a sheet with Avery's knife and tying Mr. Scudder up while they held the gun on him. Tony and Avery tied his hands behind his back and tied his feet, and put a gag on his mouth. He didn't try to fight them.

Then Tony West pulled the gag down and started asking him questions, like "What's your name?"

I remember them asking him if anybody else was in the house and he said "Yes, Joey."

From the minute they started with the knife, and cutting up the sheet and tying him, I was crying and scared to death. Joey Wells was scared too, or he told me he was. I said, "Please let's go. Don't hurt anybody. Just rob them if you're going to, but don't kill anybody!"

Tony West looked at me and Joey and said, "Shut up! This is just a way of life. You got to do things to get by."

I said, "You don't have to do these things."

As they were tying him, Mr. Scudder told Tony and Avery that they didn't have to do this. He said, "I'll go along with your game. What kind of game do you want to play?" I think he was still hoping it was all some kind of joke.

I was begging Joey to take me out of there. He took me down the ladder and we took off running down the road. I just remember running down this dark road with Joey right behind me. I heard shots and Joey yelled out, "Stop or Tony will shoot us." Tony had come after us with the gun. He was angry because we ran and told us to stop running and go back to the chicken coop. We went back but stopped at the car. Tony got in and tried to crank it but it wouldn't crank so he said, "Let's go in back in there." He made us go. I said I didn't want to, and I was crying. I was afraid of that man and stayed close to Joey. He said he'd shoot us if we didn't go back, so we did.

Avery was holding the knife on Charles Scudder. I don't

remember Scudder saying anything. He didn't beg for his life or anything. Maybe he thought it was all a game or that it would be over soon after they robbed him. Tony gave Avery the gun and Avery said, "Well, I'll go down and get rid of that man and the dogs." We heard four or five shots in a little bit and then Avery came running back up and said, "I've killed the dogs, and I've killed the man."

Mr. Scudder started moaning and crying when he heard Avery say that. Avery made him get up and helped him down the ladder. Joey and I went next and then Tony with the gun. We all went in the house and Avery went first, taking Mr. Scudder.

The first thing we saw was the body (of Joey Odom) lying in the hall in the kitchen. Tony told Joey, "Cover her eyes. Don't let her see." But it was too late. That poor man was lying in so much blood. So much blood... A big pool of it all around his head. I glanced at him once and saw he had a beard, I think, and his hair was all covered in blood. I tried to cover my face, so I don't remember exactly what he looked like. I didn't want to see.

But Mr. Scudder...when he saw Mr. Odom's body on the floor...He was trying to get to the body and crying and moaning and yelling. It was the worst thing I ever heard. He was in so much pain, and I can still hear the sounds he was making. He wanted to kneel down beside Joey Odom, but they wouldn't let him. It was so awful. They pulled him away and we all had to step over Mr. Odom's body to go to the library. As we went in there we saw where Avery had shot the two dogs. They were lying by the stove, all bloody too.

When we got in the library, West pushed Mr. Scudder down on the couch and asked for his money. He kept asking him about valuables in the house, over and over. From the time we came down to the house until Tony shot Mr. Scudder was about thirty-five minutes. At one point, Tony was trying to get Mr. Scudder to talk, but when he kept shaking his head, Tony got frustrated and said, "Get me a soldering iron."

Mr. Scudder said, "I don't have one. There's no electricity."

Author's Note: In later interviews with investigators, Avery Brock would say that Tony West wanted to "stick the soldering iron up his 'tail'" to make him talk and say where the money was hidden. They had planned this ahead of time.

Mr. Scudder stood up one more time and tried to walk with his legs still loosely tied, He walked toward the place where Mr. Odom was lying, half in the kitchen and half in the dining room. He was trying to get to him. West yelled for him to stop. But he kept going, still looking at Mr. Odom and crying. That's when Tony shot him for the first time with the rifle. The shot went right between his eyes. I can still see that bullet hole if I close my eyes. There was blood trickling down onto his nose and his mouth, but he never made a sound.

I was terrified. I was looking down at the poor dogs, because I couldn't bear to look at Mr. Scudder. I was sick from the awful smell of the blood and the heat from the wood stove—I can still smell that blood sometimes—and I wanted to get out of there and run as far and as fast as I could away from that place, but I couldn't. I knew that Tony and Avery would kill me if I tried.

It was then that Charles Scudder looked over at me, the blood still coming from his forehead, trickling down his face, and he said, "Teresa, are you all right?"

This was the most amazing thing to me. This poor man, already fatally wounded, and probably knowing he was about to die, asked me if I was all right. Maybe that's why I felt and still feel such a strong connection to Charles Scudder. It's hard to explain if you've never experienced anything like it before. I was standing in front of him watching the blood coming from the wound on his forehead, and he was talking to me, asking me if I was okay.

It was odd, too, because I don't remember ever telling him my name. He may have heard someone say it, but if he did, I was not aware of it.

I said, "Oh, please don't worry about me. You just be worried about yourself. Just go along with what they tell you to do and maybe they won't hurt you anymore."

That's when he shook his head and said, "I asked for this."

Tony and Avery both were acting so mean and aggressive. Tony pushed and shoved Mr. Scudder backwards and he fell back in a chair. He got up again and tried to go the few steps into the dining room where Mr. Odom lay. Tony shot him in the forehead two more times with the rifle. Tony looked up and said, "Now tell me, by God, that I don't have the guts to kill somebody."

Incredibly, Mr. Scudder tried to get up one more time to go to Mr. Odom. He fell down to his knees but he was still trying to talk. He made a kind of gurgling sound, and Mr. Scudder fell down near

Mr. Odom's body. After all those shots he finally lay still.

I just remember the room being so hot that I thought I was going to faint. I wanted to go outside because the smell of the blood was so horrible. I told them I had to get out or I'd be sick. Joey and I went in the kitchen and stood by the open door, and finally Tony said we could go outside for a minute and made Avery take a gun and go with us. Tony told Avery to look for valuables. He kept saying he was going to be rich when he left there and that he knew there was money somewhere in the house. He said he'd be happy the rest of his life and never have to ask anybody for anything, just like he was going to be a millionaire or something when he left. They just knew there was money there, but as far as I know they didn't find anything but some change.

Crime scene photo, showing the ransacked bedroom.
Note the bed pictured on the left—this is the antique bed belonging
to Scudder.

Then Tony came and told us to help them search the house and take things to the car. At one point Tony got me alone in a room and made a pass at me. He said he wanted to have sexual relations with me. I was sick and just wanted to get away from him, not to mention the fact that I was terrified of him and he disgusted me. I said "No, I'm with Joey." I was afraid he would touch me, but he went away. I really hated everything they did that night, but that's certainly among the worst things that I remember.

They made us go upstairs and look around. The (spiral) staircase went around and around in that dark house. Avery was going through all the drawers and throwing clothes on the floor. There was a huge bed, really dark wood. There wasn't much light up there and I don't remember clearly, but I think there were lanterns. I don't think they found anything much when they searched. Tony put on a leather jacket he found and they talked about taking the gold harp, but decided it wouldn't fit in the car. Avery went to look at Mr. Odom and said, "The son-of-a-bitch is still alive. I got to finish him off!" He put the pistol he found upstairs down to Joey Odom's forehead and shot him again.

Author's Note: They left with only a handful of dimes and nickels, bits of jewelry, including Charles Scudder's bracelet, silver candelabras, and a gold-plated dagger. The gold harp was too large to take with them. They also took Scudder's black CJ-5 Jeep with white pentacles painted on the doors. According to Joey Wells' statement to law enforcement, Avery had turned the car around to shine the lights into the house. They went back inside and found a pistol and a set of handcuffs. They were loading the car when Avery noticed Joey Odom still breathing. Avery then made the remark about him still being alive and fired the pistol at his forehead. According to the coroner's report, Odom was shot five times both by a rifle and a pistol. Odom was shot once at close range with the pistol, as if the pistol had been pressed to his skin.

When they finished looking all over the house and didn't find much they were angry. I was just numb at that point, but still very afraid of those two men. Avery started talking about burning the house to hide any evidence but Joey Wells said, "No, it will draw too much attention on top of the mountain like this. Somebody will come up here." I punched his arm, because I was praying for the Lord to send the law up there.

Tony and Avery kept talking crazy, saying they were going to live in a castle one day. Avery said he'd just live in this one because "nobody ever comes up here. These men don't have relatives."

I remember saying I wanted to go home, because I had a little girl at home. Tony West said, "I have five little boys that I never get to see."

I said, "Well, that's not my fault." I still think he would have killed me too, if Joey hadn't been a relative of his. It was a blessing I survived at all that night.

After the valuables were put in the car, the men were able to jumpstart the Javelin. Joey and I were in the Javelin, driven by Tony West and Avery got into the Jeep belonging to Scudder and he drove it. We went straight back to Joey's mother's house, and all the way Joey kept telling me not to tell his mother. I remember feeling threatened, and scared to death.

On the way down the mountain, Joey told Tony to take the jacket off so his mother wouldn't see it. Once we got down and back to Joey's house, Tony said for me not to tell the law or he'd come back and kill me.

I still tried to get Joey to go to the law once I got him alone and he said, "No, I'm not going to tell on my uncle." When the other men left, I asked Joey to take me back to LaFayette. I needed to go home to my daughter.

Myra, Joey's mama asked me if something was wrong, but I shook my head no. It's funny because I can't remember much about those days I stayed there after the murders. It's like I was in a daze and I slept a lot. Joey didn't want me to leave. I was surprised to learn later that they actually took me back home that same night to pick up my child, but stayed with me the entire time. I have no memory of that at all, and for years I agonized over leaving my child alone at my friends' house. It was during the research for this book that testimony from Lamar Blevins, one of the friends I left my daughter with on December the twelfth, came to light. He told investigators that Joey Wells and Myra Hopgood brought me home that same night to pick up my daughter. He said I appeared to be upset and distraught. I believe now that I must have been in a state of shock.

I don't remember much about the next couple of days, but I know I was at Joey's house. I think Joey may have told Myra to keep me there. I stayed there for several days until one day Joey was playing cards at a neighbor's house. Joey took me with him. They left me alone and I got to a phone. There was no phone in Joey's house. I called a friend who came and got me. He took me to my parents' house. I told my uncle what happened and he said we'd go to the law. Joey came over to my uncle's house and we talked. That's when I told Joey I was going to the law with him or without him. That night we called the sheriff.

Chapter Seven

"What about Phelps? Was he a devil too?"

The murder of Lt. Kirby Phelps

Photo Credit: Find a Grave website

The next victim of Avery Brock and Tony West was a Navy lieutenant named Kirby Key Phelps, aged twenty-six. This shocking, senseless murder committed while the two were on the run occurred at a Vicksburg, Mississippi interstate rest stop. The account of the murder would sicken and shock juries in both Mississippi and Georgia. Phelps was murdered on December 14th, only two days after the murders of Scudder and Odom.

After the murders, Brock and West had decided to run. West

93

sold their red Javelin to Myra Haygood for seventy-five dollars, though she could only give him seven dollars at the time, so they were low on gas money, not having scored the big haul they'd hoped to at Scudder's residence. West arranged for his sister to send him the rest of the money, and he and Brock returned the rifle to Brock's mother's house. The killers left Georgia, headed toward Mexico.

Navy lieutenant Kirby Key Phelps had just completed a two-week training course at Mayfield Naval Station near Jacksonville, Florida. He was on his way to his next duty station in San Francisco, California and planned to stop by Oklahoma City on the way to visit his mother for Christmas. He got sleepy while driving and stopped at a rest stop on Interstate 20, near Vicksburg, Mississippi.

In an evil twist of fate, Brock and West had stopped at the same rest stop. They slept for a while and when they awoke, they noticed Phelps' brown 1980 Toyota parked nearby with a single occupant. Needing money, they rapped on the window and then forced their way into Phelps' car and ordered him to get out. They took thirty-three dollars from his wallet.

Phelps said, "Take anything you want but please don't shoot me."

West fastened handcuffs on his wrists and marched him to a pine thicket about two hundred yards behind the rest stop. Meanwhile, Brock unloaded everything from the Jeep into Phelps' car.

When West tried to cuff Lt. Phelps to a tree, the lieutenant took a swing at him, and West fired three shots at Phelps' head, killing him instantly. Later, when the district attorney questioned West about why he shot Phelps, he asked, "Was he a devil too?"[20] (Referring to West's earlier statement in court that he had killed Scudder and was glad he'd done it because Scudder was a devil)

West said, "I wouldn't have killed him if he hadn't taken a swing at me."

West took Phelps' wallet and went back to the rest stop, leaving the body in the woods. Once back at the cars, West followed Brock, who was driving Phelps' car, and they abandoned Scudder's Jeep near Tullahoma, Louisiana. The killers continued on to Austin, Texas in Phelps' Toyota.

According to what West and Brock said in interviews with the G.B.I. and on the witness stand at their trials, West and Brock had driven from Georgia to Mississippi and then on to Austin, Texas, where they picked up a hitchhiker, who showed them where a pawn shop was. Tony pawned Phelps' camera and stereo for two hundred and fifty dollars. They rented a motel and went out drinking and to a topless bar. Tony wanted to go to Mexico, but Brock objected to the plan. They argued and split up later that night back at the motel. Brock said he had a date, and told West not to let the hitchhiker spend the night, but West did anyway. They argued and West left in the car they stole from Phelps, abandoning Avery Brock and leaving him stranded in Texas. West reportedly told Brock, "Get lost. I'm going to Mexico without you."[21]

Brock then hitched rides from Austin to Marietta, Georgia, where he surrendered to police on December 20th. He had first called his mother, Betty Jo Lowrance, when he arrived in Marietta and told her to come get him. "I didn't do it, Mama. Tony did it," she reported him as saying.[22]

It's interesting to wonder what those people who gave Brock all those rides in their vehicles back home to Georgia must have thought about if and when they learned of his arrest. This cold-blooded, unrepentant killer, who had already killed Lt. Phelps for *his* car and left a trail of bodies from Georgia to Texas—why hadn't he simply taken one of their cars? Did he have some kind of symbiotic relationship with Tony West, killing only when they were together?

Two agents back in Chattooga County, who reported they had a "gut feeling" to return to Mrs. Lowrance's trailer, noticed when they arrived that she was acting nervous and uneasy. They questioned her to find out what was going on and she told them about Brock's call. They sent the Cobb County authorities to pick up Avery Brock. He was arrested without incident and a necklace and ring, belonging to Charles Scudder, were found on him and taken into evidence.

West stayed in Austin a few more days and then headed back home, taking a circuitous and seemingly aimless route that finally brought him back to Chattanooga. One of the investigators had stated earlier as they were searching for the men that "They'll come back home. Guys like them don't fit in anywhere else."[23]

By this time, Warren County Mississippi authorities had found Phelps' body in the wooded area behind the rest stop on Interstate 20. It took another week for the Navy to identify the body as Lt. Kirby Phelps. He was found with three .22 caliber bullet wounds to the head and with a pair of "cheap handcuffs" attached to his wrists.

It didn't take long for F.B.I. investigators to discover the bullets were from the same .22 caliber pistol that was used to shoot Joseph Odom in Georgia. Louisiana agent Patrick Lane testified at the one of the trials that they found Charles Scudder's Jeep abandoned about ten miles outside of Vicksburg off I-20, near Tallulah, Louisiana.

Prints from the vehicle matched those of Tony West. A bloody footprint found on a pillowcase in Corpsewood matched a boot print found in the Jeep as well. The boots belonged to Avery Brock.

The late-model Toyota the defendant stole from Lt. Phelps was found on a street in Chattanooga, Tennessee. Tony West had abandoned the vehicle after it ran out of gas in the rain near 23rd Street around midnight of the night he turned himself in.

West had walked to a nearby bar after the car ran out of gas. He walked up to a police officer and told the officer he was wanted for murder in Chattooga County. At first there was some confusion about whether or not there was a warrant for his arrest. When the police officer he surrendered to checked for warrants, there weren't any. The warrants had been issued for Samuel West. Still, the officer detained West, took him to the police station and called Georgia to verify finally that, indeed, warrants did exist.

When the Rossville, Georgia sheriff went to pick him up at one a.m. West was wearing a three-piece suit that had laundry markings for Lt. Phelps. In addition, he was wearing a bracelet bearing the name *Charles*. He confessed freely to wearing the murdered lieutenant's clothing and of taking the bracelet off the body of

Charles Scudder.

Chapter Eight

"All I can say is that they were devils and I killed them. That's how I feel about it."

The Trials

It is definitely worth noting that the majority of people who were living in Chattooga County, Georgia during this time were shocked and sickened by the murders of Charles Scudder and Joey Odom. Even though defense attorneys for the murderers tried to blame the victims by alleging drug use, drunken orgies and strange occult practices by the victims, the jurors remained unconvinced. One of the potential jurors was asked if he thought being on drugs was an excuse for the murder and he said he thought the excuse was a "cop-out." The jury also rejected the idea put forth by one of the defense attorneys that Scudder had a motive to drug the men "because he was a homosexual." The jury is to be highly commended for not being drawn into such blatantly homophobic rhetoric.

Charles Scudder and Joey Odom did receive justice, and for a small conservative southern community, some thirty years ago, to find the defendants in the trials guilty as charged sent a strong message to the world.

Tony West and Avery Lowrance Brock were convicted of murder in Georgia and in a subsequent trial in Mississippi. Both men signed confessions admitting their crimes in both states, and admitted guilt again in interviews with the investigators, but each man accused the other of firing the fatal shots that killed Odom and Scudder. In fact, Brock even tried to implicate one of the eyewitnesses, Joey Wells.

Kenneth Avery Brock told investigators a completely different story from that of both eyewitnesses and Tony West, blaming most of the shooting on West. In an interview by Tony Gilleland, he admitted going back to the car and getting a rifle, but said that when he came back to the chicken coop, Tony West was already holding the professor at knifepoint.

Tony pecked on the door with the gun barrel. Joey come to the door, and he seen the gun and he took off running around the end— well, the kitchen through the dining room and Tony shot four or five times through the window as the door was coming open. He hit Joey about two times in the head and cut—well, knocked the kerosene lantern of the wall in the process.

He continued, "Joey fell down and we took the professor around into the dining room. We stepped over Joey, walked into the living room and Tony had the professor by the hair of the head with the gun stuck in his side. When the dogs ran around the left side of the living room, Tony shot both of them and killed them."

The investigator interrupted with a question—"Had he already

100

shot the dogs?"

"Yes, one time apiece."

"Through the window?"

"No, when the door swung open."

"Before or after he shot Joey?"

"Before."

"Okay."

"He shot the dogs twice and then Joey. Joey fell and we went on in the living room. He pushed the professor down on the couch, started going through drawers and stuff, and I was walking through the house, drinking wine and looking at the sterling and brass. The professor got up and started to walk to the dining room and Tony shot him two or three times. He fell down against the cabinet or bookcase rather and he was still breathing, but Tony didn't notice it and we went ahead and got a bunch of the stuff and put it in the Jeep."

"Okay."

"We come back in and Tony heard the professor breathing and he shot him two more times. We got more stuff and I heard Joey breathing...or air bubbles coming up, with the blood coming out of his throat and I shot him in the top of the head with a .22 caliber pistol."

"Then what happened?"

"I went out, crunk (sic) the Jeep up and cut the lights on so it was facing the house and they was still standing in there. I went in to see what they was doing and they was looking for money in the

cookie jars and flour boxes and stuff but they didn't find no money.
So, I told them, let's go and we went out."[24]

Later in the interview, Gilleland asked how long they had been planning to rob and kill Scudder and Odom:

"About three days before."

"Three days?"

"Me, Joey and Tony planned it."

"You, Joey and Tony, when you say that, who do you mean?"

"Tony West and Joey Wells."[25]

It should be noted that Joey Wells was questioned and released on December 18th by Special Agent C.W. Johnson, Sheriff McConnell and District Attorney Ralph Van Pelt. Joey Wells was never charged with any crime. Joey's sworn statement was much like Teresa Hudgins'. He said that he was drinking wine and that Avery and Tony were sniffing toot-a-loo. He confirmed that Avery went to get the gun, that he pulled the knife on Scudder and that when he and Teresa ran, Tony West came after them. He told them he couldn't let them go and they would all leave together. Joey said he pleaded with Tony not to hurt the professor, but that Tony said, "It's just a way of life."[26]

Joey Wells said it was Avery who went down to the house with the gun. He said he heard Avery yell at someone, presumably Joey Odom, to "get the dogs and get out here." He then heard about four or five shots. They then took the professor down to the house and he sat on a chair and Teresa sat with him. The professor got up and Tony told him to sit down. The professor was then shot by Tony four or five times. He said the professor fell to his knees and then up against the bookcase. Joey said they made him and Teresa help them search the house and told them that if they told the police, Avery and Tony would say they were involved too.

Avery turned the Jeep around and shined the lights inside the house. He found a pistol and a pair of handcuffs. Joey Wells said the professor moaned at that point and Avery said, "The son-of-a-bitch is still alive" and shot him with the pistol.[27]

Joey Wells further stated that later that week Teresa called him and told him she was going to the police, so they got together and called the sheriff.

****

The defense attorneys were court appointed, and since both West and Brock had signed confessions and there were eyewitnesses to the crime, these attorneys faced an uphill battle from the start. The first man to be tried was seventeen-year-old Avery Brock. Brock continued to allege he was not the shooter. He claimed he had only given one *coup de grâce* to Joey Odom when he came back in the house to load up the loot and found him still making sounds. He claimed it was Tony West who killed Charles Scudder and fired the other shots at Joey Odom.

After damning testimony was given against him at the hearing, he was indicted by a Georgia Grand Jury on February 9th. After consulting with his lawyers, Brock decided to take a plea. His attorneys stated that if the judge had given him the death penalty they would have taken the plea off the table. However, the judge sentenced Brock to serve three consecutive life sentences, and on February 15th, Brock pled guilty to the murders.

In a statement given on December 21, 1982, Avery Brock tried to pin most of the blame on Tony West and tried to implicate Joey Wells by saying he'd helped them plan the murders three days before the crime. Later, when the judge asked Brock during sentencing what happened, he said, "I killed Odom. Odom was the first one to die. I shot him through the front door, in the temple twice. Then when we come back to the house...Scudder got up and started walking toward the dining room and Tony shot him five times in the back of the head. We loaded up the stuff, got in the Jeep and the car and left. We went from there to Mississippi."

"Was it a planned matter?" asked the judge.

"Yes sir," Brock replied.[28]

Brock was taken to the Floyd County jail and later transferred to Alto Correctional Facility in Alto, Georgia.

Tony West was tried separately and it soon became apparent to his defense attorneys that there was more evidence against him than Brock. West had already confessed to the murder of Lt. Phelps to every law enforcement officer who had questioned him. West was indicted in February and the jury selection got under way on February 28th, Superior Court Judge Joseph E. Loggins presiding. More than ninety percent of the potential jurors admitted to having read newspaper articles about the case.[29]

In brief opening arguments, the assistant district attorney gave a summary of the evidence against West. When Skip Patty, the defense lead counsel, gave his opening statement he put the idea forward that his client had been given a dose of LSD-25 involuntarily in a glass of wine given to him by Dr. Scudder. His contention was that the murder was not premeditated.

"Something bizarre happened up there," he said. "We submit to you that this might have been an experiment with LSD that ran amuck." He stated that Dr. Scudder was involved in LSD experiments in his lab at Loyola (a charge that his co-workers later disputed).[30]

The first witness for the State was a friend of the victims, Raymond Williams. He stated that he traveled to Corpsewood on December 12th to inform the couple that a mutual friend was ill in a Rome hospital and not expected to live. On December 14th, Williams returned to inform them of the death of their friend. "The Jeep was gone so I thought nobody was there," Williams testified. I returned on December 16th and found the bullet holes in the kitchen door window." Williams left and went to a neighbor's house to call for help. Williams further testified that he had never seen any drugs in the residence and that he was a frequent visitor.[31]

The next witnesses showed grisly crime scene photos. Mrs. Fiumefreddo, Joey Odom's sister, quietly cried during as the photos were shown and there was speculation of how Joey Odom had been shot as he tried to run away. The defense attorneys noticed and reported it to the judge. They were afraid it would prejudice the jury against their client, so the judge said it would have to stop. He said he would tolerate no emotional outbursts in his courtroom.

There was also testimony that the two victims had eaten supper only a short time before they were killed. Friends said they normally ate at five o'clock each day. The murders were said to occur a little after seven p.m., on the evening of December 12th based on the autopsies. Ballistics evidence and information about the Mississippi murder were also given.

Eighteen-year-old Teresa Hudgins at the time of the trial

Eyewitness testimony was given by Joey Wells, describing what he saw. Wells said he waited to go to the law about what he'd seen because "they might have thought I had something to do with it." The next day, in front of a packed courtroom, Teresa Hudgins gave her testimony, along with the arresting officer of Tony West. Her testimony was a match to that of Joey Wells in most respects.

At around this time in the proceedings, Tony West became agitated, standing up and saying, "I don't want to play anymore."[32] He was subdued by deputies and a recess was called. After more damning testimony from investigators, the state rested its case.

Later that day, West took the stand in his own defense. He said the LSD-laced wine had driven him insane. Claiming that he and Brock had been given a different bottle of wine than Teresa and Joey (a fact that the others disputed), he said he had only a hazy recollection of the subsequent events, and he felt dazed and like "he was in another world." He said he shot the dogs, not Avery Brock, because he "thought they were lions." He said he saw the furniture grow larger and described walking to the car and seeing the trees "glowing" around him.[33]

At this point the defense asked for a mistrial because they overheard a juror in the front row say West "sure did have a good memory for someone so high on drugs."[34] The motion was denied.

Mrs. Tracy Wilson, a local resident and sometimes visitor to Corpsewood, testified next, stating that she had once had a small cup of wine at the Scudder residence and had "felt funny." The judge denied attempts by the defense to allow testimony from Mrs. Wilson that "Scudder could make people do whatever he wanted," and that he was conducting experiments in Summerville as a continuation of his work in Chicago.[35] Much of her testimony was not allowed.

West's court-appointed psychiatrist stated that West "seemed very capable in discussing the events of the night of the murders." The psychiatrist said West was "not psychotic" and never mentioned drugs to him.[36]

During the trial, Dr. Karczmar, Scudder's close associate in Chicago and a co-author on many scientific studies with Scudder, was contacted by authorities for an interview. In the telephone interview Karczmar made a sworn statement that to his knowledge, Scudder was not a drug abuser nor a devil worshipper, and that he was dependable. He also said that to his knowledge, Scudder never did any research with LSD and that he seemed to have been the type of person who disapproved of drug use.

Avery Brock was brought to the stand the next day to testify for the prosecution. He said that he had drunk the wine from the same bottle, and suffered no such ill effects as West described. He said he didn't believe it had any drugs in it. He wouldn't elaborate on much of anything else because he said he was going to have "another trial," so he had to be careful what he said.

Brock refused to testify against West when he was called as a rebuttal witness. "I ain't gonna answer that," Brock said repeatedly as Van Pelt asked him sixteen different questions. The questions ranged from his home address to who pulled the trigger on the weapon that killed Odom. Asked by Judge Loggins why he would not answer, Brock said, "I have another trial coming up and I'm not going to damage myself with it."[37]

David Pace, an Associated Press reporter, gave this description of the exchange between the prosecution and the defense over the likelihood of drugs being given to the killers as the trail drew to a close. His report stated, "The jury was faced with determining whether West plotted the robbery and slayings or was 'involuntarily intoxicated' by drugs during the crime. West's attorney, Clifton Patty, contended during the Chattooga County Superior Court trial that Scudder, a former college drug researcher, spiked wine he gave West and Kenneth Avery Lowrance Brock, seventeen, of Walker County, with a mind-altering drug such as LSD. Several vials marked 'LSD' were found in Scudder's home, authorities said."

The prosecution argued the claim of involuntary intoxication was a smokescreen for the cold-blooded murders of Scudder and Odom. Brock pleaded guilty to murder and armed robbery and was sentenced to three consecutive life terms in prison. Judge Loggins told the jurors they should find West innocent if they decided that, "because of involuntary intoxication, he did not have sufficient mental capacity to distinguish between right and wrong." Loggins said a person can be considered involuntarily intoxicated if he consumed alcohol or drugs through "excusable ignorance" or through coercion or fraud by another person.[38]

"We don't have to prove anything in this case," defense attorney Patty said in his closing argument Tuesday. "But in this case we have proved that there was some reason that the state hid that LSD."[39]

In actual fact, the state did not hide the LSD evidence. It was sent to the Georgia Crime Lab and found to be pure LSD-25. However, the lab said the sample was old and didn't appear to have been opened before they opened it for testing. The wine was tested for LSD and no trace was found, but the evidence was ruled inadmissible because of a technicality over how much time the defense would have had to counter the evidence.

"Just suppose that Dr. Scudder used this wine to get Avery to have sex with him." Patty said to the jury at one point. "Then after Avery didn't like it, he tried to use drugs to influence him to continue. This doctor *(Scudder, who had his PhD, not a medical degree)* knew how to use LSD, knew how to mix drugs and knew how drugs affect people. He had a motive because he was a homosexual."

Assistant District Attorney Ralph Van Pelt said the killings were premeditated as part of a robbery and that "Tony West is the one who had the unmitigated gall as to wear the clothes of the man he had murdered." Referring to the drug defense, Van Pelt said, "It's a man trying to save his own skin with the reddest herring you have ever seen. That's all this LSD business is, a red herring." Van Pelt asked the jurors to consider why West, when he was making a confession to Georgia Bureau of Investigation agent Charlie Johnson, "didn't say anything about the furniture growing or the dogs looking like lions" as he testified in his own defense. "He had made no statement about him being drugged."

"They didn't ask. They didn't ask," West yelled out from his seat at the defense table.[40]

David Pace also described the scene when the jury brought back the verdict. "Samuel T. West sat at the defense table smoking a cigarette and showed no emotion as the court clerk read the jury's decision....The seven-woman, five-man jury deliberated an hour and forty-five minutes before reaching the verdict on two counts of murder and one count of robbery."[41]

West was put in leg irons and taken from the courtroom. As he left, West was stopped by reporters in what had become, according to Chattooga County investigator Tony Gilleland, a daily press conference. West told reporters, "That man drugged us at that castle, and I'm going to find some way to prove it."[42]

West was brought back in for sentencing after lunch. Tony West was sentenced to die in the electric chair on May 2, 1983. The judge said, "May God have mercy on your soul, Samuel T. West." West lit another cigarette. He was taken to the Floyd County jail and later transferred to Jackson Diagnostic Center, which houses an electric chair.

Not having the right number of women on the jury led to grounds for an appeal and a retrial for West, which resulted in his guilt being reaffirmed by the new jury. During his second trial he was sentenced to three consecutive life sentences.

Tony Gilleland said, "It causes me, in the deep recesses of my mind, to question our system of justice. More than $100,000 dollars spent to convict two men in two states for three cold-blooded murders, after both had signed confessions admitting to these heinous crimes."[43]

Tony West faced trial three separate times for the murders of Joseph Odom, Charles Scudder and Lt. Phelps. According to a 1988 newspaper article by Pamela Purcell, the Mississippi Supreme Court reversed the decision of a lower court, because according to Warran County District Attorney Frank Campbell, the judge had "interjected himself too much in the case." The article reported that this was the second time the death penalty in the case had been reversed. The first time the Supreme Court of Mississippi ruled that the prosecution linked West to the "devil-worshipper" case in Georgia and that evidence of other crimes was inadmissible. West had been sentenced to die in the electric chair in Chattooga County and of three consecutive life sentences in Polk County at his second trial. He was then tried for the third time in Mississippi where the conviction was upheld. Tony West was sent back to Georgia to serve the life sentences.

While in jail, Avery Brock attempted suicide. He was unsuccessful and later sent to a Georgia prison. West is currently serving out his life sentence at Augusta State Medical Prison. Brock and West have been denied parole multiple times, and remain incarcerated to this day.

Teresa Hudgins fears that one day they might get out, which is one reason she chooses to keep her last name and her current location confidential. Teresa remembers that time in her life as chaotic and frightening. At one time, she was offered witness protection for herself and her child, but after learning she would never be able to return to the only place she'd ever known and would never have been able to contact anyone she knew ever again, she chose not to take it.

She and Joey Wells both were closely guarded during the trial. Teresa remembers that she and Joey were taken to the old Sheraton Hotel in nearby Rome, Georgia, for the duration of the first trial and sentencing. They were given separate rooms and police were stationed outside their doors. Teresa and Joey were not allowed to leave and were told to order room service for meals. It was overwhelming and frightening for Teresa to be in a situation like this, and to realize she and Joey Wells had to be guarded so closely. It's one of the reasons she is still so circumspect about guarding her identity, even today.

Chapter Nine

"If you gaze long enough into an abyss, the abyss will gaze back into you."

Aftermath

Photo Credit: Find a Grave website
The marker for Charles Scudder
Forest Home Cemetery Marinette County, Wisconsin
Ashes buried in family plot.

Joseph Odom's ashes scattered in the rose garden at Corpsewood,
Trion, Georgia

Dr. Scudder's and Joey Odom's bodies were cremated in Chattooga County in the days following the murder. A small funeral service was held at Corpsewood for both men but eventually, Scudder's ashes were sent back to Wisconsin to his sister, Janet Scudder Arnold, despite Scudder's avowed wish to have his ashes scattered at Corpsewood. Scudder's ashes were buried in the Scudder family plot on April 25, 1983.

Joey Odom's ashes were claimed by his sister, Mary Fiumefreddo, and on January 19, 1983, Odom's ashes were scattered in the rose garden at Corpsewood Manor after a small service for both men.

On January 5, 1983, the chicken house was destroyed by fire. Arson was suspected.

Dr. Scudder's gold-encrusted harp and a bronze statue of Mephistopheles from Corpsewood fell into the possession of locally famed defense attorney Bobby Lee Cook of Summerville, Georgia by 1986, perhaps in payment for his services. Cook had been hired by Scudder's sons Fenris, Saul, and Gideon Scudder to represent their claim to the estate.

Scudder's sons had laid claim to the $75,000 estate left by Scudder. Joseph Odom's sister, Mary Fiumefreddo, along with her two other sisters, had also claimed the estate, as Scudder's will had left everything to Odom. Mrs. Fiumefreddo was represented by Summerville attorney Arch Farrar, Jr.

A probate hearing was conducted by Judge Jon Payne at the Chattooga County courthouse in February following the murders. It was closed to the public and the press. Teresa Hudgins and Joey Wells were called to testify as were several forensic and crime lab specialists. Judge Payne ruled that Scudder predeceased Odom, but that Odom was given the final *coup de grâce* from Avery Brock with the revolver. Bobby Lee Cook appealed the case to the Chattooga County Superior Court.

The dispute was over who died first, Scudder or Odom. Though the evidence was inconclusive, Judge Payne said he tended to find with Odom's relatives, because Scudder had specifically stated he didn't want to leave his estate to his sons in his will.

Judge Loggins presided over the appeal. There was a great deal of discussion over the Simultaneous Death Act in Georgia. Scudder's relatives contended that the facts of the murders showed either that Odom predeceased Scudder or that the sequence of deaths could not be determined, thus necessitating the application of the Simultaneous Death Act. Since Odom had no children, they contended, the result of either of the above determinations was that Scudder died intestate, and that they, as his heirs, were entitled to inherit and administer his estate.

Although the court acknowledged that circumstantial evidence can be sufficient to establish the fact that two deaths were not simultaneous, and, thus, sufficient to avoid the operation of the Simultaneous Death Act, the court nevertheless found that the evidence in this case was insufficient as a matter of law. The court therefore applied the Simultaneous Death Act, and ruled that Scudder's property passed to the Scudder's relatives by intestacy.

Fiumefreddo, Odom's sister, appealed. As a result there was a great deal of attention given to who died first, and some of this is most interesting testimony. We present here a part of the discussion by the court.

In the evidence presented to the court, were testimonies given by Dr. James Dawson and Kelly Fite at the probate hearing. Dawson, the Assistant Director of the Georgia Crime Laboratory, observed the crime scene and performed autopsies on the bodies of Scudder and Odom, which were discovered four days after the murders. He testified that Scudder died of gunshot wounds to the head and that he removed four .22 caliber bullets from Scudder's head. He also testified that Odom was shot five times in the area of the head behind the left ear, and that he removed five .22 caliber bullets from Odom's head. Based on the evidence gathered from the crime scene and the autopsies, he concluded that he could not determine which of the victims died first.

Kelly Fite, a firearms examiner with the crime laboratory, testified that he examined both a .22 caliber rifle recovered from the car driven by one of the murderers and the bullets which Dawson removed from Scudder and Odom. He was of the opinion that the four bullets taken from Scudder were fired from the rifle, and that of the five bullets removed from Odom, two were fired from the rifle, two were more than likely fired from the rifle, and one was not. He testified that the latter bullet was a .22 caliber short bullet, whereas the others were .22 caliber long rifle bullets.

There was evidence that on December 12, 1982, Tony West,

Kenneth Brock, a/k/a Avery Lowrance, Teresa Hudgins, and Joey Wells went to Scudder's home in Chattooga County. Scudder's property contained both a main house, in which he and Odom lived, and a guest house. Teresa Hudgins testified at the probate hearing, and both she and Joey Wells were subsequently deposed for purposes of the appeal to the superior court. Teresa Hudgins testified that, when she and the other three approached Scudder's house in their car, Scudder came out of the main house and escorted them to the guest house, where Scudder was tied up with sheets, and where Lowrance obtained a .22 caliber rifle. Scudder was asked who was in the main house, and he replied that Odom was. Hudgins said that Lowrance then left the guest house; that shortly thereafter she heard several shots; and that when Lowrance came back to the guest house about ten to fifteen minutes later he said that he had killed the man in the main house. Hudgins testified that, with Scudder still bound, they all then went to the main house, where, after entering the house through the kitchen door, Hudgins saw Odom lying in a pool of blood.

Hudgins testified that approximately thirty-five minutes after Odom was shot, West shot Scudder several times with the rifle, and that Scudder fell beside or close to Odom. She said that after Scudder was shot, Avery and West searched the house, and loaded their car with certain valuables. According to her testimony, Scudder began moaning and gurgling blood before they left, and Lowrance, taking a .22 caliber pistol he had found in the house, said that he was going to finish him off. She said that she could see

Lowrance as he was standing near the bodies, and that Scudder and Odom were both lying close to him. She said that she heard two shots fired but that she could not, from where she was sitting, see the bullets hit anyone. She also testified that these last pistol shots were fired about thirty minutes after Scudder was first shot. She said that Odom did not move or exhibit any signs of life while she was in the house.

Hudgins was also questioned concerning the position of Odom's body. She initially said that, when she first went in the main house, Odom was lying mostly in the kitchen, near a pool of blood on the kitchen floor, and partly in the dining room area, which separated the kitchen from the library. She subsequently testified that when she left the house Odom was lying completely in the dining room area, with his head near the entrance to the library and his feet near the entrance to the kitchen. Crime scene photographs show the body lying in the latter position in a pool of blood on the kitchen floor. Despite these indications of a shift in the position of Odom's body, Hudgins also said that she never saw Odom move, be moved, or show any signs of life, and that his body was located in the same position when she entered the house as when she left the house.

Author's Note: Teresa was outside the house for a short time because she was feeling sick. This could account for not seeing Odom move. Also she testified that she was crying and frightened. At times she hid her face. She still says that if Odom moved, she never saw it.

The salient points of the testimony of Joey Wells concern his recollection of the position of Odom's body and of the identity of the man Lowrance shot with the .22 caliber pistol. Wells maintained that, when he, West, Lowrance, Hudgins, and Scudder went to the main house from the guest house, Odom's body was lying in the dining room area between the kitchen and the library. Upon being shown several crime scene photographs, he stated that Odom's body was in the position shown in the photographs when he first entered the main house and when he left.

Wells also stated that he was sure that Lowrance fired two pistol shots into Scudder, but that it was possible that the pistol was shot more than twice. He stated that he heard Scudder gurgling, and that Lowrance shot him with the pistol to finish him off. Moreover, he said that Odom did not gurgle, move, or show any signs of life while he was in the house. However, in a statement given to the police on December 17, 1982, five days after the killings, Lowrance said that the black-haired man (Odom) started moaning and that Lowrance shot him with the pistol. In response to being confronted with this statement, Wells said that he was sure the last two shots were fired into Scudder with the pistol, and that Scudder was the last one he heard moaning, but that his December 17 statement could also represent the way it happened.

It was up to the court to sift through all the evidence and the at times conflicting testimonies. This is what they finally decided:

We must now determine whether the trial court, on the basis of the above evidence, properly granted summary judgment based on the Act. We agree with the appellees that many inferences in favor of the conclusion that Odom predeceased Scudder can be drawn from the above evidence, namely, that Odom was shot several times in the head some thirty minutes before Scudder was shot, that Scudder was the victim who was gurgling blood and was shot with the pistol, and that Odom did not move while Hudgins and Wells were in the home. However, because the appellees were the movants for summary judgment, the evidence must be construed most strongly against them, and the appellant must be given the benefit of all favorable inferences and all reasonable doubts if the evidence is ambiguous or contradictory. Construing the evidence in light of these principles leads to the conclusion that the grant of summary judgment was improper.

As for which victim was moaning and gurgling blood and was shot last with the pistol, the evidence presented was ambiguous and contradictory. However, based, first, on the physical evidence, which showed that only Odom had been shot with a .22 caliber short bullet, and second, on Wells' December 17 statement to the police, it is inferable that Odom was the victim gurgling and moaning, thus prompting the last pistol shots from Lowrance. On this summary judgment action, we must give the appellant the benefit of this favorable inference. Hudgins' testimony concerning the position of Odom's body was also contradictory, indicating on the one hand that he was lying mostly in the kitchen, and on the other that he was lying in the dining room. Although she may be mistaken about seeing Odom lying mostly in the kitchen, we must resolve this ambiguity in favor of the appellant for purposes of this summary judgment action, and doing so leads to the inference that Odom moved at some point while Hudgins was still in the house or after she left, and is consistent with him being the victim who was moaning and gurgling. Because the above inferences indicate that Odom survived Scudder and that survivorship might be determinable, we conclude that the trial court erred in granting summary judgment based on the Simultaneous Death Act.[44]

Before anyone could take possession of the house, it was burned to the ground by persons unknown. Some of the more valuable items in the home had already been removed and were saved from the fire.

Avery Brock today
Photo Credit: State of Georgia Prisons

Tony West today

Photo Credit: State of Georgia Prisons

Chapter Ten

Haunted Corpsewood?

Dead Horse Road on an early summer day
Photo Courtesy of Corpsewood Manor: A Castle in the Woods
#pariahprose

In the weeks and months following the murders, many people visited the estate, tromping through the gardens and taking small "souvenirs" like bricks and garden sculptures from the residence.

Some people even dug up plants and flowering bushes. Later, residents would claim the souvenirs from the crime and house were cursed and had brought them bad luck.

Even during the police investigation, officers reported a feeling of being watched and of a "strange presence" at Corpsewood. People visiting the site still report shadows and apparitions believed to be Odom and Scudder. Voices, gunshots, barking dogs, and shattering glass—as well as haunting melodies played on Scudder's golden harp—have all allegedly been heard on the property.

After nightfall, some witnesses have claimed to see the glowing eyes of Beelzebub, one of Scudder's mastiffs, staring at them from the woods. It is said that it's dangerous to be at the site after darkness falls, and one local author and medium, Mark Fults, describes the homestead as "unexpected and beautiful" but also "dangerous." "The property is deceiving," he said. "It's idyllic, but there are people out there who use it for bad things. Places that have trauma sometimes attract more trauma. It's easy to get deceived that it's a safe place." There have even been reports of people conducting satanic rituals after dark. Now, as in 1982, the curious and the predatory still pay visits to the area.

It's certainly possible there is some truth to the stories. According to paranormal investigators, tragic, violent events always increase the probability of a place being haunted. And spirits who have not been affected by such events generally have no problem "crossing over to the other side" or moving on. Those who are the center of such an occurrence feel bound to this world until they receive some form of justice, retribution, or simply someone knowing their personal stories of sorrow. Violent deaths, cruelty, and abuse are some of the most prominent events that bind a ghost to the earthly realm. Certainly violence and cruelty happened at Corpsewood.

However, there are also reports like these, taken from some of the blogs and websites that are still actively questioning whether or not the site is haunted:

From a public post by Paul Cagle of the South Eastern Paranormal Society, posted April 14, 2008: *I have actually been to Corpsewood Manor. My paranormal group and I have been several times to investigate the site. Unfortunately, we have never gotten a picture, EVP or even EMF spike at this location. The only two things that happened was we got one brief temperature drop and something did follow us out, both times that we left. The two round buildings which were the well and the chemical toilet are still standing but most of the walls have been knocked down and the structure has been gutted. I've had friends that told us of seeing spirits pointing from the gazebo out into the yard, and spectral hands pulling at clothing when they exited the woods. It was so peaceful the two times that we went, that I could have gone to sleep with no problems in the structure.*

And this from a post on March 3, 2009, by an anonymous author: *I am a member of a paranormal research team from the Atlanta area. I have been to Corpsewood once, several years ago. The claims some people have made we did not witness first hand. In fact, nothing out of the ordinary really happened at all. It is an interesting and very sad story, but I personally don't think it's haunted. I do believe that based off the fact that so much of their own personal energy and love was put into the land, there may definitely be some residual energy there, but I don't personally believe their spirits haunt the land. I believe and hope that those two men have crossed and gone to wherever they are supposed to be. What happened to them was horrible and inexcusable. I plan on going back in the future to see if we can try it again and put some evidence to the stories.*

Should anyone believe the stories of paranormal activity? Judge for yourself. There are several good books and many blogs written about Corpsewood that put forward claims for supernatural events occurring on the property. There are numerous videos on sites like *YouTube* that show the results of paranormal teams' investigations.

The public's attraction to sites like Corpsewood and fascination with the idea that the living could contact the spirits of the men who were murdered there could simply be a kind of morbid curiosity. This is according to Eric Wilson, professor of English at Wake Forest University in North Carolina, who argues his case in a new book called *Everyone Loves a Good Train Wreck: Why We Can't Look Away*. In his book, he says, "There are many reasons why we're attracted to the morbid. It's titillating, and it's a weird physiological arousal, an animal stimulation—some scientists even think it has an evolutionary value. We learn what not to do to get caught up in the same experience."

Professor Wilson further states, "This was something that the renowned psychologist Carl Jung believed in. Jung might say that we have a shadow side. Most of us go through life repressing it, yet it draws us to death and gore. But Jung says it's psychologically healthy, because it can help us get to know ourselves. Morbid curiosity allows us to think about the meaning of suffering and death."

"The key, though," says Professor Wilson, "is using imagination to try to make the suffering meaningful, to learn something from it and not become obsessed by it." He says, "If we open up empathetically to the other person it can make us more human."

Chapter Eleven

Reflections

"By three methods we may learn wisdom. First, by reflection, which is noblest; second by imitation, which is easiest; and third, by experience, which is the bitterest."

—Confucius

Friedrich Nietzsche once famously said, "If you gaze long enough into the abyss, the abyss will gaze back into you." Charles Scudder and Joseph Odom were often imprudent about sharing their lifestyle with a community that was friendly and willing to welcome newcomers, but still extremely conservative. The good people of the area, and there are many, were mostly accepting of the men and appreciated their friendliness, even if they didn't agree with their lifestyle. Unfortunately, not everyone who visited Corpsewood had good intentions. Scudder was gregarious and outgoing, used to the atmosphere of a much more liberal metropolitan college campus. His eccentric interests would have been much better kept private. The very peace and privacy he said he craved was destroyed by sharing too much with his neighbors. Perhaps Charles Scudder realized this far too late when he said, "I asked for this."

Tony Gilleland, a chief investigator for the Chattooga County

129

Sheriff's Department said later in an interview with a Summerville newspaper that he was "deeply affected by the case." When asked to write his thoughts for the newspaper article, he said, "I have no doubt of their guilt," (referring to West and Brock). "The first two victims' only crime was to welcome people into their home. The last victim's only mistake was to become tired while driving home for Christmas."[45]

Lt. Phelps' tragic error, then, was parking his car in an isolated rest area to sleep. And Charles Scudder and Joey Odom were too friendly and too open about their lifestyle and beliefs in a place that was simply too conservative to handle them. Teresa Hudgins has declared she made a mistake in going with the three men she barely knew that night despite her misgivings and a small voice inside her telling her not to get in the car. There is a lesson to be learned in all these cases about being more vigilant in the increasingly violent world we live in, but this book's intention is not about blaming either the victims or the eyewitnesses. Their roles in all this were tragic and heartbreaking.

According to what Dr. Juliana Breines says in a recent article in *Psychology Today*, "Victim blaming is not just about avoiding culpability—it's also about avoiding vulnerability. The more innocent a victim, the more threatening they are. Victims threaten our sense that the world is a safe and moral place, where good things happen to good people and bad things happen to bad people. When bad things inevitably happen to good people, it implies that no one is safe, that no matter how good we are, we too could be vulnerable.

The idea that misfortune can be random, striking anyone at any time, is a terrifying thought, and yet we are faced every day with evidence that it may be true."

Dr. Lerner theorized that "these victim blaming tendencies are rooted in the belief in a just world, a world where actions have predictable consequences and people can control what happens to them. It is captured in common phrases like "what goes around comes around" and "you reap what you sow." We want to believe that justice will come to wrongdoers, whereas good, honest people who follow the rules will be rewarded. But this happiness may come at a cost—it may reduce our empathy for those who are suffering, and we may even contribute to their suffering by increasing stigmatization. What the world may lack in justice we can at least try to make up for in compassion."

These victims, Scudder, Odom and Phelps are deserving of our compassion and our sympathy. Victim-blaming attitudes only reinforce what the killers said all along: that it was these victims' fault these murders happened, when in actual fact, it was *not* the victims' fault or responsibility; it was the killers' choice. By engaging in victim-blaming attitudes, society allows murderers and abusers to perpetrate their crimes while avoiding accountability for their actions.

As for the murderers themselves, they were young men who were drifting through life, with no roots and no purpose. Both men were extremely poor, with not even any power or running water in their trailer home, but both men were young and able-bodied, capable of finding jobs that could have led them out of poverty. Could their greed have blinded them to what was right to the extent that they placed no value on the lives of Scudder, Odom, and Lt. Phelps and simply decided to take whatever they wanted?

What does it take for a person to kill another human being? The answers are unclear, but experts say that most killers are easily frustrated, with limited or poor impulse control. They frequently express anger or hostility and believe violence and aggression are legitimate responses to various personal problems in life. Although they might never admit it, pleasure or reinforcement is derived from the expression of anger (i.e., it feels good to blow someone off; it makes you feel alive; it gives you a sense of power). West's statement to Teresa Hudgins after he shot Charles Scudder is an example: "Now tell me, by God, that I don't have the guts to kill somebody."

Killers often display the characteristics of a "stimulus seeker." They engage in bold, fearless, or reckless behavior and are prone towards substance abuse. Tony West was in trouble for most of his life because of his reckless, angry behavior. He and Brock were both substance abusers and both were men who responded to problems with violence.

In addition, killers like Tony West often believe things are easier for everyone else, that other people get more and have more advantages. Brock seemed to resent Scudder and Odom for their lifestyle and their home, not considering how hard the men had worked to build the place by hand. They talked of just moving in after they killed Scudder and Odom and taking the "castle" for themselves.

Also consider Tony West's erratic behavior during his trial. At one point, he jumped to his feet and yelled, "I don't want to play anymore." He gave daily press conferences during his first trial and complained that no one understood what happened to him. Again, according to psychological studies, killers like West wallow in their "victimization" and are psychologically impotent to deal with their anger.

Summerville, Georgia and the other small municipalities in the area, like Trion, which is nearest to Corpsewood, remain small, quiet towns in the Northwest Georgia Mountains, not far from Tennessee. According to its official website, the people of Summerville, and indeed the entire area, "exhibit warmth, friendliness and helpfulness to their neighbors and visitors." Certainly this is all true. But in December of 1982, it would also be the scene of a horrific murder, one that captivated residents of the normally placid town where church buildings almost outnumber businesses even to this day.

Chapter Twelve

Epilogue

It seems fitting that this story should end as it began with the words of Teresa Hudgins herself and her reflections on these tragic events and on her life as it unfolded after the murders. Like the ancient mariner in the poem by Coleridge, who tells his "ghastly tale" to those who need to hear it, Teresa once felt compelled to tell her us her remarkable story, but now she hopes she can put it behind her forever. This is her ending, which in many ways, is only a beginning:

After I called the sheriff that night, I went in to his office. After talking to me, the sheriff called in the Georgia Bureau of Investigation, and they came and asked me questions for hours. They gave me a polygraph test that same night. The GBI investigator told the sheriff, "There's no way that girl is making any of this up."

I testified at both trials and at the trial in Mississippi. I was the only witness to come forward willingly. Joey Wells told the investigators that he didn't like to tell on anybody, and I don't know if he would have come forward if I hadn't told him I was going to. I personally don't think he ever would have.

It was terrible to sit in that crowded courtroom, with everybody

134

staring at me. I was so close to Tony West, and he was looking right at me. I was still terrified of him, and the investigators and the district attorneys all told me not to even look over at him, but just to keep telling the truth. That's exactly what I did.

Since I turned state's evidence, I had heard rumors of people coming after me, and I thought sometimes I was followed. I look back on it now and wonder how I did it. I was only eighteen years old.

That night of the killings, before Tony West left he had told me that he would kill me if I went to the law. I was scared the whole time, and I still wonder if one day they'll get out of prison and come looking for me. I've been told they'll never get out, and I truly hope that's so.

I really wonder if I had been able to somehow stop from telling what I knew, would the murderers have ever come to justice? I haven't seen or heard from Joey Wells since the events of the murder and trial, and I have no idea what happened in his life. I received a plaque from Chattooga County law enforcement commending me for my courage and for coming forward. I still have it hung in my home today.

I still suffer from the things I witnessed. I dream about them sometimes. After my testimony in court, no one heard much from me or about me, and there has been speculation and rumor as to why I was even on the mountain that night, and why I waited several days before coming forward with my story. Maybe this account has explained a bit about my life and how I came to be on Taylor's Ridge that night.

I have things in my past that I can't and won't ever talk about. Things that would hurt people close to me if they came out. But it's time I moved on from those old hurts, like I want to move on from that awful night in 1982, and I really believe that I have.

I began to move on from it all when I travelled back up to Corpsewood in 2006. An author contacted me and said he was writing a book about the murders. He asked me to go with him to the scene and tell him what I remembered. I checked him out and agreed to go with him, but I was reluctant to go at first. It was one of the few times I'd been back there since that night.

Once we walked back onto the property, however, I saw how beautiful and quiet it was, and I was glad I'd come. It was early in the morning and the dew was still on the grass and in the trees. I sat down on the ground, and I don't know why, but I felt the presence of Charles Scudder there around me quite strongly. I raised my head to look up at the trees and I began talking out loud to him, telling him how sorry I was for what had happened to him in that place and how I was sorry that he lost his life.

Tears were falling softly from my eyes and running down my face as I spoke to him, and I told him that I wish there had been something I could have done to help him that night, all those years ago. All of a sudden, I noticed this one big tree in front of me. The wind had picked up and was blowing through the treetops, but out of all the trees in that clearing, only the limbs of this big tree were dancing in the breeze and none of the others. The sun came out and shone directly down on the tree, and at that exact moment the tree branches shook hard and rained all the dew right down on top of me. The light was shining on the drops and they were silver in the sun and fell all around me and over me. It felt like a benediction.

Trees on Corpsewood Property

I felt a shiver go over my entire body and this strange feeling shot all through me from head to toe. In that moment I felt peace radiate through me, and I said, "I've got my peace. He's letting me know he doesn't think any of it was my fault."

I knew then that Charles Scudder is up there on the mountain with Joey Odom. I think he's there still on the land he loved so much, or maybe he comes and goes when he wants to or when there's a need. I felt his presence on that day, and I think it was because he was letting me know he didn't blame me for anything. I knew then that I'd never be afraid of that place anymore.

I've come to realize that there was nothing I could have done that night to change the outcome. Tony West and Avery Brock were two men, violent killers, who were not going to be controlled by a young teenaged girl. I feel very fortunate that they didn't kill me too. But what I could do for Charles Scudder and Joey Odom was to tell my story and maybe help in some way to clear their names and set the record straight. They lived a different lifestyle from me and from most of the people in Chattooga County. But I don't believe they were devil worshippers. They were kind men, not hurting anybody, and I hope this book has helped to show that in some measure.

My youngest daughter, whom I'll call Erin, came to me while she was still in middle school, all excited because she had found the old news magazine that told about that night in 1982, and she was curious to know all about it. I told her a little then, but felt she was too young to know all of it. Later in 2013, she and I traveled back to Corpsewood, and she got to see it for herself for the first time. I tried to use it as a teaching moment, to stress to her how careful she has to be and to remind her to always trust herself and her own feelings about things. If I had trusted my own feelings back then, I might never have gone to Corpsewood, and never had to witness what happened that night. I felt good about showing it to her and while I didn't have any experiences up there that time, I still felt the same sense of peace deep inside.

As for what happened in my life, I have children and

grandchildren. I went to work for a while with inmates at a prison in a nearby county, working as a supervisor in food services. I met a wonderful man there named Matt. He was my boss and the Director of Operations. We were only friends at the time, but years later, when I was transitioning between jobs, and waiting and hoping for a special job that I really wanted to come through, I contacted him again. I texted Matt to see if he knew of any openings at my old job. He didn't, but then later he called me and we spoke about what I'd been doing since I'd seen him last. His wife had passed away, and he was still single, but wore his wedding ring after some six years. I was impressed by that. I told him about the writing of this book and he was surprised. He hadn't realized I was the same Teresa who witnessed the crime. Matt wound up coming over to pick me up to talk about it, and we went to a Mexican restaurant. We talked and made plans to see each other again, and we've been seeing each other every day since. So in a way, this book helped bring us together.

I had an awesome opportunity around that time to travel to Colorado to visit my youngest daughter. For the first time I flew in an airplane, even taking my little Chihuahua with me. It was such a great experience and helped me even more in getting over my fears. After I came home, I found that the job I wanted had come through, and I'm really happy now with my life. I work hard every day at a job I love, and I have someone in my life who loves me and who wants to take care of me.

I survived an event that has plagued me over the years, and I hope now to be able to let it go, and put it in its place. I'll never forget it. But I have stopped letting it influence the way I live. Charles Scudder and I were strangers whose paths crossed for such a short time on that one night in December, after which we would be forever linked. Charles Scudder and Joseph Odom lost their lives that night, and in a sense, I lost a part of myself. Certainly, my life has never been the same. I often wonder how things might have been different for me if I had never gone up to Corpsewood with Joey that night.

I am finally happier than I've been in years, and I look forward to what the future will bring. I hope that this book will also give me some degree of closure. Before a person can live out her dreams, she must first realize what her dreams are. I'm happy to say I'm not afraid anymore.

The End?

.

ABOUT THE AUTHORS

Shannon West currently lives in the South with her husband and family. She began writing them a few years ago and now has over fifty short stories, novellas, and novels to her credit. She was a finalist in the Rainbow Awards in 2013 and 2014, and very honored to be an All Romance Ebooks Top Ten Author for 2013 and 2014. She mostly spends her days at the keyboard, trying to elude housework, which stalks her relentlessly.

Susan E Scott is the bestselling author of more than twenty short stories, novellas, and novels. She lives with her husband in a small town in north Georgia. Susan and her husband are both owned by their Yorkie, Sophie, who is the undisputed queen of the household.

<u>CITATIONS</u>

[1] "Cherokees In Chattooga." N.p., 26 Nov. 2011. Web.

[2] Find A Grave. N.p., 31 July 2013. Web

[3] Scudder, Charles. "A Castle in the Country." Mother Earth News Mar.-Apr. 1981: n. pag. Print.

[4] Budd, James, ed. "Murder at Corpsewood." Summerville News Apr. 1983: n. pag. Print.

[5] Find A Grave. N.p., 31 July 2013. Web

[6] Budd, James, ed. "Murder at Corpsewood." Summerville News Apr. 1983: n. pag. Print.

[7] Budd, James, ed. "Murder at Corpsewood." Summerville News Apr. 1983: n. pag. Print.

[8] Budd, James, ed. "Murder at Corpsewood." Summerville News Apr. 1983: n. pag. Print.

[9] Budd, James, ed. "Murder at Corpsewood." Summerville News Apr. 1983: n. pag. Print.

[10] Budd, James, ed. "Murder at Corpsewood." Summerville News Apr. 1983: n. pag. Print.

[11] Budd, James, ed. "Murder at Corpsewood." Summerville News Apr. 1983: n. pag. Print.

[12] Budd, James, ed. "Murder at Corpsewood." Summerville News Apr. 1983: n. pag. Print.

[13] Budd, James, ed. "Murder at Corpsewood." Summerville News Apr. 1983: n. pag. Print.

[14] Shankbone, David. "Satanism: An Interview with Church of Satan High Priest Peter Gilmore." Wikinews. N.p., 5 Nov. 2007. Web.

[15] Shankbone, David. "Satanism: An Interview with Church

of Satan High Priest Peter Gilmore." Wikinews. N.p., 5 Nov. 2007. Web.

[16] Budd, James, ed. "Murder at Corpsewood." Summerville News Apr. 1983: n. pag. Print.

[17] Budd, James, ed. "Murder at Corpsewood." Summerville News Apr. 1983: n. pag. Print.

[18] State v West. Superior Court of Chattooga County. Mar. 1983. Print.

[19] Budd, James, ed. "Murder at Corpsewood." Summerville News Apr. 1983: n. pag. Print.

[20] Budd, James, ed. "Murder at Corpsewood." Summerville News Apr. 1983: n. pag. Print.

[21] Budd, James, ed. "Murder at Corpsewood." Summerville News Apr. 1983: n. pag. Print.

[22] Budd, James, ed. "Murder at Corpsewood." Summerville News Apr. 1983: n. pag. Print.

[23] Budd, James, ed. "Murder at Corpsewood." Summerville News Apr. 1983: n. pag. Print.

[24] Investigative interview with Chattooga Law Enforcement

[25] Investigative interview with Chattooga Law Enforcement

[26] Investigative interview with Chattooga Law Enforcement

[27] Fiumefreddo v Scudder. Supreme Court of Georgia. 1984: Web

[28] Budd, James, ed. "Murder at Corpsewood." Summerville News Apr. 1983: n. pag. Print.

[29] Budd, James, ed. "Murder at Corpsewood." Summerville News Apr. 1983: n. pag. Print.

[30] State v West. Superior Court of Chattooga County.

Mar. 1983. Print

[31] State v West. Superior Court of Chattooga County. Mar. 1983. Print

[32] State v West. Superior Court of Chattooga County. Mar. 1983. Print

[33] State v West. Superior Court of Chattooga County. Mar. 1983. Print

[34] State v West. Superior Court of Chattooga County. Mar. 1983. Print

[35] State v West. Superior Court of Chattooga County. Mar. 1983. Print

[36] State v West. Superior Court of Chattooga County. Mar. 1983. Print

[37] State v West. Superior Court of Chattooga County. Mar. 1983. Print

[38] State v West. Superior Court of Chattooga County. Mar. 1983. Print

[39] State v West. Superior Court of Chattooga County. Mar. 1983. Print

[40] State v West. Superior Court of Chattooga County. Mar. 1983. Print

[41] Budd, James, ed. "Murder at Corpsewood." Summerville News Apr. 1983: n. pag. Print.

[42] Budd, James, ed. "Murder at Corpsewood." Summerville News Apr. 1983: n. pag. Print.

[43] Budd, James, ed. "Murder at Corpsewood." Summerville News Apr. 1983: n. pag. Print.

[44] Fiumefreddo v Scudder. Supreme Court of Georgia. 1984: Web

[45] Budd, James, ed. "Murder at Corpsewood." Summerville News Apr. 1983: n. pag. Print.

Made in the USA
Columbia, SC
13 January 2021